William Naphy is Senior Lecturer and Director
of Teaching and Learning in the School of Divinity,
History & Philosophy at the University of Aberdeen.
He is the author of *Born to be Gay: A History of Homosexuality*,
co-author of *Plague: Black Death & Pestilence in Europe* (both
published by Tempus), *Plagues, Poisons and Potions*, and general
editor of Tempus' *Dark Histories* series. He is a regular guest on
Radio 4's *Start the Week*, and has been historical consultant
on Channel 4 and BBC TV documentaries on the history
of plague and witchcraft. He lives in Aberdeen.

SEX CRIMES

From Renaissance to Enlightenment

WILLIAM NAPHY

TEMPUS

*For Arlene, Donald,
Paul & Ruth*

First published 2002
This edition first published 2004

Tempus Publishing Limited
The Mill, Brimscombe Port,
Stroud, Gloucestershire, GL5 2QG
www.tempus-publishing.com

© William Naphy, 2002, 2004

British Library Cataloguing in Publication Data.
A catalogue record for this book is available from the British Library.

ISBN 0 7524 2977 9

Typesetting and origination by Tempus Publishing Limited
Printed in Great Britain

CONTENTS

ACKNOWLEDGEMENTS

As with all such exercises, it is impossible to thank everyone who played a part in the production of this volume. However, first and foremost, I must offer my gratitude to Jonathan Reeve, publisher at Tempus, and the entire publishing house for their encouragement in this project. It would almost certainly have never been undertaken without their support. Also, I express my appreciation to the British Academy, the Carnegie Trust for the Scottish Universities, and the Economic and Social Research Council, whose generous grants allowed the research into many of the criminal cases used in this book. Finally, I would thank two friends (Andrew Spicer and Diane Balaguer) who suffered through years of listening to my accounts of sex in the early modern world and another friend (Sean Bothwell) who kindly read parts of the manuscript. His comments were most helpful though, obviously, all errors remain my own.

W.G. Naphy
Aberdeen

I

Illegal Sex

one

FORNICATION AND CELIBACY

The control of sexual activities was of paramount concern to every society from the Renaissance to the Enlightenment no more and no less than to societies and cultures before and since. Despite variations over time and from culture to culture, the reality is that there was a widespread consensus. Sex, except within marriage and then normally in the missionary position, was undesirable (at best) and illegal (at worst). The primary purpose of sex was the procreation of the human race. Acts which did not promote this goal were unnatural. However, even sex that did have the potential to produce children was monitored and controlled. Any production of children beyond the confines of marriage had consequences for a society and, therefore, was of concern to that society. With extreme emphasis placed on inheritance, paternity, male honour, and the patriarchal control of female sexuality, these societies invested heavily in the regulation of sexual behaviour.

This volume will look at the range of sexual acts controlled by societies through an examination both of general views on sex, gender and sexuality as well as a consideration of specific crimes which exemplified these ideas. Basically, non-marital sex was understood in two ways. First, as will be discussed in Part One, there were sexual acts which had the potential to produce children but which also threatened the fabric of society and its economic and cultural underpinnings. Fornication (sex by unmarried men and women), celibacy (the promotion of abstinence as better than marriage), adultery (sex in which one or both individuals is already married), bigamy (being married to more than one person at a time), rape and violent sexual assault, and prostitution will be examined in some detail. In their participants (that is, one man, one woman) and sexual 'positions' these types of sex were broadly 'heterosexual' (to use the modern word). Nevertheless, people were regularly and often severely punished for involvement in these activities. More importantly, the presuppositions (the theories) and the consequences (the practice) of these acts varied from the Renaissance to the Enlightenment. Moreover, socio-cultural views about these variations of 'normative' sexuality differed markedly from those held today.

In the second part of this volume, 'unnatural' sexual acts will be examined. While the behaviour discussed in the first part of the book was often punished harshly – executions were known for adultery, rape and prostitution, for example – the participants in the acts detailed in the second part of this work were almost always risking death. This section will look at 'non-procreative' sexual variations: for example, adult men with adult men; adult men with adolescent males; child abuse; women with women; masturbation; sadism; group sex;

bestiality; and sex with demons and Satan. Again, it will be important to stress those changes in socio-cultural views over time from the Renaissance to the Enlightenment. In addition, the presuppositions which underlie the responses to these sexual acts and their variation from the views of today (which might result in similar responses but for different reasons) must be examined.

In general, the greatest threat posed to the control of sexual acts in the early modern period (broadly understood as c.1450–1800, depending on the locale) was female sexuality. Representing half the population, women were a grave threat to the patriarchal control of society. Women alone had absolute assurance about their relationship to their children. They knew beyond a shadow of a doubt that a child was their own child. Husbands and fathers lived, unhappily, with the awareness that they could never absolutely ensure that the children to whom they would leave their worldly possessions and who would sustain their line and honour were actually their progeny. This lack of assurance meant that, at all cost, female sexual activity had to be monitored and controlled to ensure paternity. Moreover, the emphasis upon male honour and female chastity (purity) meant enormous stress was laid on controlling female sexual activity from birth to death.

The real problem faced by these societies was that the men viewed women as extremely dangerous and sexually vora-cious. Daniel Rogers, in *Matrimonial Honour* (1642), spoke for almost everyone in the period in every culture when he said,

> And if we but consider the nature and qualities of the
> generality of that sex, even in all ages from the fall of man

unto this present, we may well perceive that they have not
been onely extreamly evil in themselves; but have also been
the main instruments and immediate causes of Murther,
Idolatry, and a multitude of other hainous sins, in many
high and eminent men.

Men were potential victims of sex-driven women. Women
were temptresses controlled by their wombs whose power
over men had led the latter into destruction and sin from Eve
onwards. The sexual depravity and physical weakness of the
female had to be controlled.

Obviously, the first line of defence against aggressive female
sexuality was the strict promotion of chastity. Indeed, the
exultation of celibacy was a logical corollary of this as it
demonstrated a generally negative view of all human sexual
activity. However, despite a medieval inheritance that exalted
celibacy over even the married state, the Reformation seriously splintered European cultural views on chastity as a voca-
tion and life-long ideal. Thus, while the Renaissance may
have shared a generally positive view of celibacy, subsequent
centuries split largely along confessional lines. Despite this
fractured view on celibacy, chastity before and outwith
marriage remained the ideal in all European societies.

Catholics remained enthusiastic about the supremacy of
celibacy and exalted it, as part of the package of religious
vows of priests, monks and nuns – as a sacrament exceeding,
in religious virtue, the sacrament of marriage. For Catholic
theology, any sexual activity remained 'second best' for the
Christian as Jerome, Ambrose and Augustine had made clear.
Cardinal Bellarmine's 'larger' catechism of 1598 explicitly and
simply states the Catholic position: 'Mariage is a thing

humane, Virginitie is Angelical. Mariage is according to nature, Virginitie is above nature'. Indeed, he is supporting a threefold understanding of human sexuality. Some acts (e.g., sodomy) were 'against nature'; some, 'natural' (sex between a husband and wife); and some 'above nature' (celibacy).

Obviously, Catholics were aware of the problems with enforcing life-long chastity and undertook reforms as part of the wider Catholic/Counter-Reformation project to ensure these vows were maintained. For the most part even here the stress was laid on the chastity of religious females. In Spain this meant that nuns were strictly cloistered having as little contact with (indeed, not even being able to see) the outside world as possible. Royal officials were given permission to examine religious communities and impose, unilaterally, alterations to their lifestyles and, even, architecture. As Ambrosio Montesino put it, 'isn't it useless to lock up nun's cloistered bodies, when their thoughts are in the courts and town'. The answer was not a re-evaluation of the celibate 'ideal' but rather the imposition of greater external measures to 'help' nuns (and male celibates) to keep their vows.

Protestants generally responded to this vaulted view of life-long chastity (especially as a religious act) with extreme hostility. They did so for a number of reasons. First, Protestant theologians largely rejected the idea that celibacy was ideal or practical for more than a very, very few individuals. Second, they doubted the ability of people to adhere to their vows and pointed to numerous actual and alleged abuses in the Catholic church. In particular (as we shall see) they focused on supposed violations of the celibate life in the confessional between priest and female penitents (an argument which also worked to support their rejection of private auricular confession) and amongst cloistered monastics – the accusations of monks' bastards being killed or abandoned to orphanages by their convent mothers are legion. In effect, celibacy simply promoted lust. Finally, they rejected the Catholic interpretation of the theological place of marriage and sex in the created order.

In defence of the latter view, Protestants pointed out that Eve was created for Adam *before* the Fall. That is, the 'marital' state was part of Paradise. Most, however, drew the line at exalting the role of 'helpmeet' to the original couple and continued to stress that the role of sex in marriage was to procreate and to avoid fornication. Though, as the next chapter will show, this view was not unchallenged.

Also, even some Catholic writers, especially humanists schooled in the ideas of the Renaissance, questioned the celibate ideal. Erasmus gave a succinct statement of this view in his *Encomium Matrimonii* (1530, English translation): 'Bachelershyp [is] a forme of lyvinge bothe barren and unnaturall'. Thus, Protestants and many Catholic humanists not only rejected Cardinal Bellarmine's third type of sexuality, 'above nature', they suggested that this type of lifestyle was actually 'unnatural'.

This equation of celibacy, its abuses, and unnatural sexuality was not unique to Protestant polemicists trying to embarrass Catholicism. A complaint by a Mayan community in New Spain (Mexico) during 1774 to the colonial government not only links celibacy and rampant sexuality but also implies an expectation that Protestantism (in the guise of the English) could rectify the problem with its emphasis on marriage and rejection of life-long chastity.

They say false baptism, false confession, false last rites, false Mass; nor does the true God descend in the Host when they say Mass, because [our priests] have stiff penises... In the morning their hands smell bad from playing with their mistresses... God willing, when the English come may they not be fornicators equal to these priests, who only lack carnal acts with men's bottoms. God willing that small-pox be rubbed into their penis heads.

Clearly, the enforcement of chastity and celibacy was prob-lematic even when buttressed by religious vows and state control. Shakespeare also viciously satirised religiously inspired chastity in *Measure for Measure*, where the pent-up sexual frustrations of Angelo, the Duke and Isabella erupt in violent punishment of sexual sinners and sadomasochism as part of their 'mortification of the flesh'.

More importantly, many aspects of early modern celibacy and its rejection expose views about sexuality in general, and women in particular, that would sit ill with modern expo-nents on either side of the argument. For example, support-ers of celibacy would undoubtedly be troubled by the more extreme mystical understandings of being 'married to Christ' expounded by some religious (especially, nuns). Thus, few would like to be reminded of Catherine of Siena's mystical marriage to Christ in which she received his foreskin as her wedding ring. Likewise, the Puritan extreme rejection of celibacy and exultation in marriage created numerous psychological tensions when they turned their attention to Christ as bridegroom and themselves (i.e., male puritans) as his brides. Edward Taylor, in a poem on *Canticles* (*The Song of Solomon*), wrote,

Thy Saving Grace my Wedden Garment make:
Thy Spouses Frame into my Soul Convey.
I then shall by thy Bride Espoused by thee
And thou my Bridegroom Deare Espoused shalt bee.

As allegorical as one might want to be, this sort of mystical focus on marriage with Christ by Catholic supporters of celibacy and Protestant advocates of marriage is (psychologically) problematic. Indeed, the logical extension of this emphasis upon Christ's marital relationship and his humanity reached its apogee (and was collectively rejected by most Protestants and Catholics) amongst Moravians under Count Zinzendorf. They openly discussed – and sang about – Christ's penis (while commemorating his circumcision) and the Virgin's womb, vagina and breasts (during Christmas celebrations). Zinzendorf even went further and argued that in eternity there was only one gender as souls were female – Christ was the sole male.

There were also practical implications of this turn away from celibacy (life-long chastity) as a religious ideal. In Protestant countries it usually meant that substantial numbers of men and women, some who had spent most of their lives in cloistered communities, were turned out into society and told to marry. For nuns this was often disastrous and unwelcome. The *Poor Claires* of Geneva, for example (with one exception) chose to relocate to a Catholic town rather than leave their independent, female-dominated, religious lives for the control of a man in marriage.

Those who chose to leave the cloisters faced the special hatred of other Catholics and often found it difficult integrating into Protestant societies especially if they had entered into relationships in Catholic countries where, by definition, they would not have been able legally to be married. In 1559, François Rouard and Ayma de Castro were arrested in Geneva for 'pretending' to be married. They had been in Chartreuse orders near Lyon (at Politain). A witness with whom they had lived for six weeks reported that François had told him that 'they were not married except by mutual consent and they had not been solemnised'. When their landlord had remonstrated with François, the former monk had said that they had wanted to make their marriage 'official' in Geneva. Instead, they were jailed for six days on bread and water and banished from the city on pain of being flogged if they ever came back.

This couple was practising a traditional understanding of marriage that was increasingly being rejected by Catholic and Protestant theologians as well as governmental authorities. Traditionally, a man and woman (assuming there were no impediments) could make promises to one another and exchange tokens as signs of intent to marry. They would then be socially free to cohabit and sleep together. At some point, they might solemnise this arrangement in a church service. As long as their families and the wider community were supportive of the new relationship this situation was largely unproblematic. However, religious and secular officials became less inclined to tolerate this situation.

First, there was widespread awareness that this arrangement could be abused, especially by men. It was often used as a ruse to convince a woman to sleep with a man. Once the sex was over or, more often, once pregnancy occurred, the woman was abandoned. Also, there was a very important legal distinction between promises that related to an 'intent to marry' (in the future) and promises declaring that the couple considered themselves 'now married'. Again, this technical distinction was something men could use to seduce credulous women. More importantly, this traditional marriage system left the basic building-block of society in the control of individual couples and their families. Reforming clerics, whether Catholic or Protestant, and governments wanted to bring this aspect of society under their control. As a result, the role of the church in marriage which had begun in the middle ages as a blessing of the marriage 'after the fact' became the only legal method of marriage. Marriage no longer represented a public declaration by a couple to live as a couple and its acceptance by their relations and neighbours; rather it became an act of the state and the church. A couple did not marry each other; they were married.

This represented a profound change to society. In practical terms it meant that anyone marrying by the traditional method was, in fact, committing a crime. Either they were fornicating or, in the delightful terminology of the time, 'anticipating' their wedding. A few cases from Geneva's copious criminal court records will suffice to demonstrate this tension in society as a long-standing cultural norm was forcibly changed from above.

In 1557, Henri Fournier and Nicolarde Guet (his wife) were jailed for six days on bread and water and fined. She had given birth a mere six months after their wedding service in Geneva's Protestant 'cathedral'. The authorities were clear that she had known she was pregnant at the time of the wedding though she was probably not visibly showing. Their investigation discovered that the couple had probably been involved for about two years before their marriage. The conclusion was that they had married the moment that she had realised she was pregnant in an effort to avoid being prosecuted as forni-cators. Sadly, they did not seem to have moved quickly enough.

The callous use of the older system of 'private' marriage seems to have been exploited, with limited success, in 1564 by François Chevallier. Jeanne Loup said that she had consented to sex with Chevallier after they had become 'engaged'. He denied that this had taken place though both admitted that they had had sex. Their relationship had been made easier by the fact that both of them worked as servants in the same house (of Claude Vandel, a leading citizen). The court decided that it could punish the crime (they received nine days in jail and a hefty fine) but was not able to decide exactly what the crime was. If Chevallier's claims were correct and no prom-ises had been made then they were guilty of fornication. If Loup was telling the truth, then they had 'anticipated' their marriage. The two were referred to Geneva's ecclesiastical court (the Consistory) comprised of leading magistrates and the entire city-state's ministerial corps. If this body decided there had been promises then Chevallier would be forced to uphold his end of the bargain.

As the decades passed, societies became somewhat more lenient towards this behaviour and, in particular, those of socially higher circles were usually exempt from the strictures of the law. In general, as long as the marriage proceeded there was little concern. The problem with private marriages was the possibility for the abuse of gullible women and the lack of official oversight. Thus, Johan and Anna Ortt (in Amsterdam in 1682) were widely known to have anticipated their marriage because her sister had told just about everyone that she had found 'soiled chemises' that clearly evidenced sexual activity. Britain's Queen Mary was somewhat less amused to find that Eleanor Franklin, one of her ladies-in-waiting, and her lover had been anticipating their wedding night. She reprimanded them both.

The case of Chevallier and Loup highlights one of the areas where fornication was easiest and chastity most problematic – the domestic household. Since urban homes of the middling sort or better had unmarried servants of both sexes as well as single apprentices and journeymen, this was a possible focal point for illicit sexual activity. Worse, it was a place where the (married) master might bring adultery into his own home. The place of adultery and the home will be discussed in greater detail in the next chapter. For our purposes here, the focus is on sex between single individuals. A cache of cases from the period of Calvin's ascendency – and, thus, of extreme religious morality – give some idea of the scale of the problem.

Philippa Noë (who was probably a widow) was Aymé Vindret's chambermaid. She admitted the moment she was interrogated that she had fornicated with Girard Cugnard, another servant in the Vindret home. Moreover, she confessed that she had been caught *in flagrante* in 1555 (three years before this trial) with Michel Baltezard by one of Geneva's leading citizens, Jean de la Maisonneuve. Because she had returned to her 'fornication' rather then repenting and, more importantly, because she had defiled her master's house, she was jailed for three days, paraded through the streets with a mitre on her head (with a picture representing her crime) while a trumpet announced her progress and, thereafter, perpetually banished from the city on pain of being flogged should she return.

In 1561, Gabriel Dunant and Françoise Coquet (a servant of Jean-Ami Curtet, syndic – one of the city's presiding magistrates) were arrested for fornication. Dunant denied the charge but admitted that he had spent five days in jail in the village of Lancy about a year before for fornicating with another domestic servant by whom he had had a child (who had subsequently died). Coquet tried to deny the charge but her position was undermined when Jeanne (widow of Maurice de la Rue) and Chrestien (wife of Antoine Lormier), mid-wives, reported that she was clearly not a virgin. She admitted that she had fornicated years ago with another servant named Abraham whom she thought now lived in the village of Orbe. Although there was no way for the city to prove their guilt (as she appears not to have been pregnant), their past crimes were sufficient to convince the city that they were unwanted. Dunant was jailed for six days and Coquet was placed in the city's pillory for three hours. They were both then banished on pain of being flogged.

The city also failed to prove its case later that year in November against Guillaume Pilligot and Jean de Monthey who were servants in the home of Antoine Revilliod. Despite close and intense questioning they both denied that they had ever had sex with each other or anyone else. He was ordered to apologise in public and never to work in the same household as Pilligot. Her case was somewhat more complex since she was also accused of singing 'dissolute songs' with some (Catholic) countryfolk while she, her master and some other servants were at his rural estate. Unable to prove either case against her, she was also humiliated in public and forbidden to work with de Monthey. It is not clear whether both or just one (or which one) had to leave Revilliod's service to obey the court's orders.

The consequences for a female servant even of being suspected of fornication is clear from a case in August 1563.

Nycolarde Clavel, a chambermaid, was arrested along with Jean Conrad, a trainee-apothecary. Both worked for Jean du Molard. They had been warned by their employer and his wife about their 'familiarity, tending towards fornication' but had paid them no heed. Nevertheless, the case could not be proven as the defendants stuck to their denials. Conrad was jailed for three days and du Molard was ordered to sack Clavel. However, that was not the end of the case. By November, it was clear that Clavel was pregnant. She then confessed that she had fornicated with Conrad (who seems, wisely, to have left town in the interim). This later case resulted in her imprisonment for nine days on bread and water. Her confession and obvious pregnancy spared her the humiliation of having her breasts squeezed to see if she was lactating or being asked the father's name while in the midst of labour.

The following year (April 1564), the trial of Estienne Bechod gives us the chance to examine the impact of a relationship between a master and servant. It is not completely clear in the dossier but Bechod may have been married. In either case, he had certainly had a child, five weeks previously, by his maid, Pollette de Corsey. He had tried to hide his crime (for which he spent two hours in the stocks) by sending her away six months previously and having the child baptised in a nearby village. However, his crime was compounded by the extremity he went to in avoiding detection. He had had the child baptised in a Catholic church with a certain Antoine Libally as godfather. It not clear what, if anything, happened to Pollette.

Thus far, the only sure proof of guilt has been pregnancy. One might think that an eyewitness would also suffice. However, the case of Jean Guet and Jeanne Fontanne proves that this was not the case. Jean Gassin and Giulio Gatty had seen Guet bathing in the Rhône one evening about 10 o'clock. Fontanna (a servant of Joseph Bouverot) had arrived with some waste to dump in the river. Gassin testified that Guet 'asked if she wanted to sleep with him later', and she had replied 'that your companions will talk if I sleep with you'. Gatty added that he had seen them hugging and Guet fondling her breasts and putting his hand up her skirt. Nevertheless, they both denied the accusations and, as there was no sign of actual sexual contact only 'familiarity tending towards fornication' the two were admonished and released.

What makes this discussion about sex and the domestic servant most interesting is both how frequent it was in practice and how noticeable it is for its absence from the literature of the period. Novels and erotic literature did not portray sex between servants and masters or among the servants. Servants are simply bit players in the narrative. Where sex between classes was portrayed, as in theatres, it was for comic effect. Erotic women (in the works largely prepared by men) were professional courtesans (not prostitutes), aristocrats (usually, 'the countess'), nuns, and young, middle-class girls who had been 'wronged'. In those few sources (for example, the writings of Giacomo Casanova) that do mention sex with servants the emphasis is very much on the exploitative, abusive and pseudo-prostituted nature of the relationship. This would seem to imply that these relationships were not perceived as erotic, rather banal. Sex with servants and between servants was perhaps too common. This may explain why the father of the Marquis de Sade's female cook was furious, not because her master wanted sexual favours from her but because he wanted to bugger her. The offence was not the sex but the unnaturalness of the act proposed.

Another area of concern in the attempt to bring extra-marital relations between the sexes under the control of church and state was the attempt to shore up parental control. By demanding parental approval, the authorities further undermined the ability of a couple to engage in a private marriage. However, as the next two cases show, couples were willing and able to attempt to circumvent not only parental control but also the oversight of magistrates and ministers. Nor were individuals unable to use the new rules to their benefit.

In 1564, Antoine Signier from the Auvergne was resident in Geneva working for Pierre Riviet. He had become involved with Françoise Tribollet, another servant in the household. They had exchanged promises of marriage. However, he tried to get out of the arrangement by presenting a letter from his mother withholding her permission. Normally, this would have been enough to get him out of the marriage though he almost certainly would have been punished (probably jailed) for fornication. Sadly for him, the court decided that the paper looked decidedly 'Genevan' and the wording too Protestant to have been written by his Catholic mother. Phrases such as 'as it pleases the Lord', 'the Lord protect you' and 'we are very happy that he is serving a man who has faith in God' were simply too evangelical. When questioned he confessed that he had forged the document (which survives in the dossier). He was publicly humiliated, forced to rip the letter in half and then sent off to the Consistory to sort out the date for his wedding.

His failed attempt to use the new approach to marriage – and Protestantism – to his advantage is in marked contrast to the behaviour of Guillaume Delestra, a leading citizen. He had left Geneva about five years before under a cloud because of his relationship with the daughter of a powerful merchant, Jeanne Marchand (who had subsequently married). He confessed that he had settled in the Tarantaise and, there, had married Marie Chambouz in a Catholic service. His parents not only had not approved, they had not known about the marriage. The witnesses were his then employer and his employer's family. He had also participated in other Catholic services. He had only recently returned to Geneva because his father needed him.

This sort of a situation was extremely complex for the city and its ministers. The youth had broken a number of laws: he had 'married' without parental consent and he had married in a Catholic service. However, he had married in a public, religious ceremony. The result of the trial highlights the diffi- culties faced by societies trying to control sexual behaviour and also instill loyalty to a specific confession. He was forced to declare his sin and apologise for his behaviour in front of the congregation in a service in Geneva's cathedral church. He was also jailed for six days and fined. Despite official wrath, the marriage was clearly accepted for we see him and his wife, Marie, presenting a child for baptism five months later. Indeed, there is no evidence that Marie suffered any punishment whatsoever.

Other attempts to circumvent the rules were even more inventive. In 1559, Jeanne-Françoise Espaule was prosecuted for using various aliases to hide her identity to allow her to live a 'debauched life' of fornication, prostitution and theft. She was flogged through Geneva's streets and banished on pain of death. Renée du Nostet was an even greater worry. She was arrested for being disguised as a boy (for which she had previously been banished) and for using a range of aliases (Supplice, Jean, Martine and Charlotte) as well as giving various places of origin. In her disguise, she had shared beds with a number of men but denied she had fornicated. She also said she was not a thief and she claimed, falsely, that her mother was a relative of Beza. She, too, was flogged through the city and banished on pain of death.

For the most part, early modern societies concluded that the best way to control sexual activities was to promote chastity before marriage. That is, a pregnant, unmarried mother was a failure for social control as much as it was a crime. What had to be controlled was, as we have seen, the type of behaviour 'tending towards fornication'. In some communities, extreme measures were taken. For example, the Moravians (whom we have already met singing about Christ's penis) opted for almost complete segregation of the sexes. In their taverns men were served by men and women by women. Women sat on one side of the church, men on the other. The community arranged marriages based on its needs and the economic skills of the putative husband and wife (to ensure they were self-sustaining). They also supported late marriages with chastity enforced until individuals were able to marry in their late twenties.

This attempt to control behaviour was also adopted in Protestant countries (and later, in Reformed Catholicism through greater use of the confessional). Geneva was held up as a model by many of how this should be done and could work. The extensive oversight provided in a city of about 10,000 souls by a dozen elders and about the same number of ministers, regular examinations, and the general lack of privacy seemed likely to produce positive results. There is a lot of evidence to suggest that, in the long run (i.e., twenty-five years) the enthusiasm for this sort of constant social control waned. However, it did manage to produce lots of cases. Many of these highlight the attempt to stop 'familiarity' before it led to 'fornication'.

Marguerite, the wife of Estienne Duval (an apothecary) was the very sort of personality the Calvinist state wanted to control. In 1561, she was arrested for her frivolous and flirtatious behaviour. She often had male friends to her house for dinner (even when her husband was away). She danced riotously, told 'inappropriate jokes and riddles', and flirted outrageously. Pernette, the wife of Claude de la Maisonneuve (a syndic), had admonished her in public. Even when called to account by the court she was unrepentant. She argued, rather logically, that she had never done anything that her husband did not know about. Thus, there was no way this could be behaviour tending towards anything. Nevertheless, she was jailed for three days and publicly humiliated and told that if she did not change her behaviour (and personality) and stop seeing her 'friends' she risked being 'convicted' of fornication whether or not sex had taken place. Thus, inappropriate interaction between the sexes could be deemed equal to fornication even without the act itself.

The same logic was used to control the character of Pernette Bressot, a widow, who was a 'teacher of girls'. She was suspected of over-familiarity with Jean Chartier, a bookseller and friend of her late husband. She had been forbidden to see him by the Consistory. This case, though, arose more from her comments during a lesson with the daughters of two Genevan ministers (Chauvet and St-André). They had been discussing proper objects for pious contemplation.

St-André's daughter said that 'wisdom and doctrine' were appropriate. Chauvet's daughter interjected the risqué suggestion that one might better contemplate 'Mon. Calvin'. Almost certainly laughing, their teacher Bressot had said, 'no, rather, Mon. Beza'. For her humour and ill-considered friendships, she was banished on pain of a flogging.

Jean Myville was prosecuted in 1565 for behaviour that was much more serious and, no doubt, bordered on sexual assault. Although assault will be discussed in more detail below, this case is interesting because it shows the difference between theory and practice in the most controlled of communities. According to Genevan rules, the sexes were segregated during church services. However, Myville was prosecuted for groping women in the press during sermons. He had so annoyed Jeanne de Roches that she had got up and left her seat to sit elsewhere. His usual *modus operandi* seems to have been to offer to share his psalm book and then to use it as a screen for his hand touching the women beside him. He also held their hands and placed his foot on top of theirs. A half a dozen women testified against him. He was publicly humiliated, branded on his forehead and banished on pain of death.

This case demonstrates a number of interesting features. Segregation of the sexes clearly did not work. Enough women must have been reasonably literate for him to think this 'book trick' would work. Also, women were extremely tolerant of low-level harassment in a public place. Finally, church services in Calvinist Geneva were perhaps more interesting than one might have expected.

Collectively, these cases also highlight the difficulties early modern societies faced as religious reformations and the increasing development of state oversight tried to control, more closely, the behaviour of the average person. Moreover, one must also be aware that the resistance was more than just from tradition and indifference. Some people actively opposed the ideas being promoted. As we have already noted, the continual use and defence of traditional private marriages was a type of resistance.

In 1553, Robert Le Moine from Normandy was arrested for his peculiar ideas. He confessed that he was not an educated man though he had had some instruction. He had come to Geneva for training in the Gospel but had not been able to go to sermons 'because of his poverty, he had to work'. He had made a joke about predestination and had said fornication (unlike adultery) was not against God's commandments. (In the sense of the Ten Commandments, he was right – a fine point lost on the court.) He had not called the minister, Reymond Chauvet (whose daughter we have already met), a false preacher and a sinner though 'he was a false witness'. He also denied saying that everyone should be equal. He was banished from the city on pain of being flogged.

Esprit Nielle was prosecuted for his opinions as well. His remarks also give us some insight into personal views on one of the ways the city tried to deal with the problems of illicit sexual activity. The city regularly raised money to care for the poor as well as orphaned (more accurately, abandoned) children. Nielle had refused, point blank, to give any money. He had said that 'he did not want to give any money to sustain fornicators and whores'. He apologised for his remarks after spending five days in jail.

Ami de la Combe had been even more vocal in his rejection of the new edicts mandating jail sentences and fines for fornication and death for adulterers. He had stood on the

Rhône Bridge with an open New Testament and read out the story of the woman taken in adultery and said '[Jesus] sent her away and who would be wiser than Him?'. Despite the best efforts of his brother-in-law to silence him he had gone on to say that 'these edicts are not good' and that 'may it please God that those who have made these edicts about fornicators and adulterers are the first to fall foul of them and they then be hung on a gibbet so high that everyone can see them'. He was forced to apologise in public and sacked from all his civic offices – in particular, as an elder on the Consistory.

One final case shows the extent of official interest in sexual relations and also makes the point that love could be an important feature of early modern relationships even in the sixteenth century, albeit being no proof against state interference. Louis Decrouz and Bartholomée Dorsières were arrested for continuing to cohabit. Their maid, Cergaz Blanc, was also punished for not reporting them. Dorsières admitted that she had been forbidden to see Decrouz even though they had lived together for quite a while. She had been widowed twice before and they had tried to solemnise their relationship (before it became sexual). However, the Consistory had forbidden the marriage because there was too great an age difference between the elderly Dorsières and the much younger Decrouz (who had never been married). There may also have been a 'class' or social distinction being made as well. Decrouz had been a servant of Dorsières' first husband (though there was no implication that they had been involved at the time). Indeed, the prohibition against the original proposal to marry 'because of the inequality between them' may have as much to do with status as age. Their determination to live as a couple proved their undoing.

As these cases have shown, women were not always likely to be punished more severely than men. However, since they were more likely to come to the attention of authorities because of pregnancy they were, of necessity, more frequently punished. The real emphasis, though, in these cases has been on the regulation of almost every aspect of contact between the sexes. This alone was seen as the way to ensure chastity, in particular, as John Corry wrote (in his *A Satirical View of London*, 1801) 'female chastity... the true foundation of national honour'. This returns us to where the chapter began. The real problem of sex was that 'women are more easily seduced than men... and soonest poysoned [by desire, heresy, and sin]' as John Eborow argued (in *The Female Zealots of the Church of Philippi*, 1637).

Women's inferiority, though, was not seen as merely a matter of physical weakness as might be meant today. Women were inverted or failed men (more on this below). In a world that saw the body ruled by its fluids (humours), women were overwhelmed by their fluids and overly full of the wrong sort of humours (hence, the need to expel excess waste each month in menstruation). As the historian Marilyn Westerkamp has said, women were 'simply soggy men'.

Not everyone was content to accept this sort of view. In fact, throughout the period from the Renaissance to the Enlightenment, there were women who strongly and loudly rejected these ideas of female inferiority and natural sinfulness. Christine de Pisan writing in the early 1400s set the tone. She identified these views with male bias and men's fear that women, if ever freed from constraints, might prove to be their equals rather than, as they claimed, their undoing. Lucrezia Marinella writing in Venice in 1600 (in her *La nobilità et l'eccellenza delle donne*) said pithily:

I wish these [detractors of women] would make this experiment: that they raise a boy and a girl of the same age [and
both fit]… in letters and in arms. They would see in a short
time how the girl would be more perfectly instructed than
the boy and would soon surpass him.

These women rejected the widely held views about their
own native debilities root and branch.

With the eighteenth century, the voices raised by women
(and, admittedly, some men) against these ideas reached a
crescendo. Mary Astell, in her *Reflections on Marriage* (1730),
wrote that women were excluded from history books not
because of their unimportance but 'because the writers,
being men, envious of the good works of women haven't
recounted their great deeds'. In response to the argument
that male strength equated to natural superiority in other
areas she replied ruefully 'and 'tis only for some odd acci-
dents, which philosophers have not yet thought worth while
to enquire into, that the sturdiest porter is not the wisest
man'. Equal sarcasm motivated the author of *Female Rights
Vindicated* (1758) to write that Aristotle's view that women
were 'imperfect men' was perplexing as 'they are deficient in
that ornament of the chin, a beard – what else [could he
mean]?'

Some men, for their part, were equally scathing about the
attempts to control sexuality – though one suspects they were
more interested in their own freedom to copulate than the
general position of women in society. Thus when Pietro
Aretino, early in our period, published his notorious *I Sonetti
Lussuriosi* (with Giulio Romano's pictures, *I Modi*, of sexual
positions) he responded angrily to attempts to censor him.

One might be tempted to see his response, and his work, as an argument for sexual liberation. However, his defence makes clear his very male-orientated, phallo-centric view:

> I am all out of patience with their scurvy strictures and their dirty-minded laws which forbid the eyes to see the very things which delight them most. What wrong is there in beholding a man possess [*sic*] a woman? It would seem to me that the thing which is given us [again, *sic*] by nature to preserve the race, should be worn around the neck as a pendant or pinned on to the cap like a brooch.

A number of exponents of the female side of the discussion, then and now, might have been inclined to suspect that most men came close to doing that in any case.

The reality was that despite active and passive resistance by individuals and the strenuous writings of both men and women, societies continued to believe chastity was essential outwith marriage. The majority of women and, in particular, parents would have agreed seeing the lack of any real ability on the part of women to control their own reproduction. However, the ideology and presuppositions underlying the promotion of chastity had little if anything to do with concern for unmarried mothers or fatherless children. As Thomas Carew wrote in *A Rapture*:

> Husband, wife, lust, modest, chaste, or shame
> Are vaine and empty words…
> All things are lawfull there, that may delight
> Nature, or unrestrained Appetite.

This was a frightening vision to most. A world without restraint given over to the fulfillment of physical – bestial – sensuality. Worse, a world in which women were free to express their sexuality. This fear explains the warning of the author of *The Present State of Matrimony* (1739): 'as to Lubricity, it is generally supposed by us, that Women are more inclined than Men. Their souls seem to be of a more amorous Temper... The Great Concern of every Commonwealth, it to keep them within due Bounds'. However, Catherine Macauley exposed the presuppositions behind male fear of female sexuality when she quoted Lord Chesterfield saying (in her *Letters on Education*, 1793) that women 'are only children of a large growth... a man of sense only trifles with them, plays with them, humors and flatters them, as he does an engaging child; but he neither consults them, nor trusts them in serious matters'. And few matters were as serious as sex; it was not something to be left to over-sexed children.

two

ADULTERY
AND BIGAMY

The insistence on chastity, especially by women, before marriage was as nothing compared with that after marriage. All of the concerns about the value of a daughter, the ability to settle her into a good match, and family honour were compounded by concerns about inheritance and the honour of both families (hers and her husband's) and, more acutely, his personal honour. This chapter will look at the rigorous attempts to control the sexual activities of wives. In addition, special attention will be given to the crime of bigamy. Early modern societies were determined to regulate who married whom as a function of both church and state. The last thing they wanted was to face the prospect not only of unfettered sex but, worse, uncontrolled and multiple marriage.

As we have already noted, the first efforts at controlling sex in marriage were directed at private engagements and marriages. The traditional idea of consensual marriage by spoken promise (not necessarily before witnesses), the exchange of tokens (of which the engagement ring is a vestige) and consummation was rejected across Europe in the course of the sixteenth century. Reformation polemicists accusing one's opponents of various types of sexual licence only accelerated the need for greater probity in supervising sexual relations and greater chastity in general. The cases of Ana García and Antonio Dovale in Spain (1672 and 1677) give some idea of the potential chaos of the customary system. Ana twice sued Antonio for making and breaking his promises of marriage, each time after the birth of a child. In this case, she was not seeking – nor was the state imposing – a punishment. Rather, she wanted financial compensation to care for the child and to recompense her for her devalued worth on the 'marriage market'.

Also, as a 1560 case from Geneva shows, individuals could attempt to use the traditional system as a cover for their illicit activities should these come to the attention of the authorities. Guillaume du Gerdil and Bernardine Neyrod were arrested for fornication. They had been caught *in flagrante* by a chambermaid. Their initial line of defence was that they were, at worst, 'anticipating' their marriage as they had exchanged promises of marriage, gifts and money. However, as it became apparent during the course of the investigation that Du Gerdil had married five years before and had had children by his wife who was still living, the judges saw this for what it was. Their summation of the case said that the customary formulae had been false, 'designed better to inflame one another to fornication' and, most offensive of all, they had both continued to attend sermons and receive the Lord's Supper. Du Gerdil, now a confessed adulterer, said that 'he had read in the Holy Scriptures that he merited death and begged God and the judges for mercy'. He was paraded through the streets with a mitre on his head while being flogged. Then he was banished on pain of being decapitated. This was despite his attempts to imply that Neyrod had seduced him 'like a whore'; no record survives of her fate.

As we have seen, the next line of defence against sexual immorality was the family and local community. In most societies a 'neighbourhood watch' scheme against adulterers operated. Anyone suspected of, or caught in, adultery could expect their home to be decorated with horns, serenaded with rude songs, and, *in extremis*, their person paraded through the village or town on an ass. This system of *charivari* was, however, open to abuse and, as most authorities recognised, outwith the control of the state. Vigilante justice – a form of traditional justice – was as unpopular with the growing state apparatus of lawyers, officials and courts as traditional marriage systems were.

However, with the cultural shift towards a greater emphasis upon affection and mutual care in marriage, a tension developed between the desire of individuals to choose their mates and families to organise marriages for mutual betterment. The *Athenian Mercury* (1691) spoke for the evolving loosening of parental control when it said, 'Parents are not to dispose of their *Children* like *Cattell*, nor make 'em *miserable* because they happened to give 'em Being'. This sensible opinion flew in the face of the need for parental permission promoted so strongly by the religious and secular reforming movements of the sixteenth century.

Moreover, the concern evidenced in the same *Athenian Mercury*, that 'he who marries a Woman he cou'd *never* love, will, 'tis to be feared, soon *love* a Woman he never marry'd', made the point that the previous stress on controlling sexual relations through arranged marriages was likely to increase the frequency of adultery while attempting to control fornication and 'anticipation'. Regardless of how a marriage was made, the families remained closely involved in the relationship knowing that any sexual immorality reflected badly on even distant relatives.

No better example of this survives than the problems occasioned for Calvin by the domestic disorder in the marriage of his brother, Antoine. Antoine's wife, Anne Le Fert, was eventually banished on pain of a flogging on suspicion of being involved with Pierre Daguet, John Calvin's servant. She had been prosecuted before for her relations with other men. Despite the use of torture she refused to confess to adultery. What is interesting is that the brothers Calvin were especially concerned that, whatever the verdict, the marriage be declared dissolved and Antoine free to re-marry. The state obliged (making obvious the Protestant acceptance of divorce, albeit in limited circumstances in sharp contrast to the Catholic rejection of the possibility).

Another family stepped in (in 1557) to stop Bernardine Neyrod (probably not the one mentioned above) from trying to run away from her husband. She admitted that she had had sex with her brother's servant, Ambroise. She had given him some money (from her dowry) and even her daughter's jewels (a coral necklace) with the intention of following him later. Her access to funds makes the point that women in Continental societies did not have their identities legally subsumed into that of their husbands. They retained limited control over their dowry and, as is still the normal tradition, kept their own names.

The important factor motivating families and wider communities to support the attempts by ministers and magistrates to control sexual activity is the one already mentioned: honour. Even more important than familial honour (which was reduced as the daughter moved from prospective bride to wife) was the honour and reputation of the husband. A husband tied to an adulterous wife was as likely to be ridiculed, as a cuckold, in a *charivari* as either of the guilty parties. This concept of honour could extend beyond the husband to the children as well. For example, the dramatic pivot of *A Fair Quarrel* (1615–17) by Thomas Middleton and William Rowley is the duel between Captain Ager and his colonel who has called Ager the 'son of a whore'. The same concern for reputation led Johan Boreel, a Dutch army commander, to have his wife imprisoned when it was widely said that she 'played the whore' and gave all her money to 'her pimps'.

The ability of a woman to destroy a man's honour was tremendous and tremendously frightening for the husband. The *Court of Good Counsell* (1607) said that there was 'no greater plague, torment... [than an] untoward, wicked and dishonest wife'. The problem was that there was so little a man could do, as all men were reminded by the author of *Tell-Trothes New-yeares Gift* (1593): 'if she meanes to deceive thee, her intention is hard to be prevented, for, watch her never so narrowly, she [will] finde a time to performe her knavery'. One edition has a dire warning in the margin: 'you cannot watch over her; though you lock her up everything and shut out everyone, the adulterer will be within'. Indeed, the very contemplation of the possibility of adultery could be destructive. *Fancies Ague-Fittes, or Beauties Nettle-Bed* (1599) noted that 'jealousie… is as irksome to beare in a man as a woman, and so much more in a man, because thereby he looseth his honour'.

However, jeopardising male honour could have more immediate and disastrous consequences for everyone concerned than social humiliation. In 1557, Marie de la Maisonneuve (of one of Geneva's premier families) was arrested for adultery with Rolet des Noyers. Everything in the trial, including a cache of love letters, pointed to her guilt. The relationship was long-standing, as was her estrangement from her husband. However, her father, Claude, was one of the city's leading Calvinists and was to serve as a syndic every four years from 1560–76. Her husband had brought the case, obviously at his wits' end. His humiliation was already complete and he now wanted her punished. He noted her familiarity not only with Des Noyers but also the city's Stews (bathhouses). Amongst her many outrageous comments that he cited he noted that once, when he was reading from Pierre Viret's *Dialogues*, he had read a passage about Leviticus 20 and adultery. She had said (sarcastically) that 'he read that to make her afraid'.

Honour and family prestige worked in two directions in this case. Her family's fame was such that the case was a *cause célèbre* in the city. Her husband, a naturalised citizen, had clearly hoped that making her adulteries public would embarrass her family into controlling her. In this case, their social status saved her life. Colladon, Geneva's chief legal advisor for much of the last half of the sixteenth century, wrote an opinion on the case. He advised that she be put to death. He must have assumed that her family's political and social prominence would protect her for this arch-Calvinist noted that

Imperial Law did allow for an adulteress to be 'confined to a nunnery'. He remarked that since this was not an option in Protestant Geneva it might be acceptable to confine her for life. The court decided to spare her but took Colladon's advice and decreed 'you [Marie] are condemned to be confined perpetually in our prisons attached to an iron chain by your right leg for the rest of your life'. In sixteenth century Europe, life imprisonment was almost unknown so one can only assume that this novel punishment was a direct consequence of the interplay of family, prestige, humiliation and crime.

In a case from 1684, across the globe in a small village (Santo Domingo Uanhuitlan) in the Oaxaca region of New Spain (Mexico) an adulterous relationship had an even more dramatic if less surprising outcome. Pedro de Caravantes, a Mixtec Indian, killed his wife (María de Montiel), rolled her in the cloak of her lover and pinned a note to her body detailing her adulterous relationship with the local sacristan, Domingo de la Cruz. For years he had suspected the two of a relationship and, eventually, had given way to his jealousy and battered her head in. The case is mostly interesting because the note was written in the local Mixtec language (in Roman letters) and allows one to hear a native speaking without the interposition of any officials or even another language (Spanish).

Both Pedro and Domingo had fled the village and could not be found. Despite the lack of the main protagonists in the story, the investigation began. A number of locals testified that a relationship had indeed existed between Domingo and María. One said the adultery was a 'very public and notorious thing' in the village. Another recalled that on one occasion an officer of the Spanish *alcalde mayor* had caught them *in flagrante* and had admonished them. On another occasion this same witness remembered that Pedro had taken María into a field, hung her from a tree and whipped her. A warrant was issued for the two men and the case languished for an entire year. Eventually, Domingo was apprehended in the vicinity of the village. He produced witnesses who confirmed most of the details already known to the court but who added that the affair had been broken off by Domingo after he had been admonished by the officer. Also, one witness recalled (at about the time of the break-up) that María had sent a letter to Domingo that the witness had had to read for the sacristan. (The implication that María was literate but not Domingo is fascinating.) In it she had threatened to end the affair if he did not assist her economically and this, along with the intervention of the officer, may have hastened the affair's end. The court decided that the sacristan could not be 'blamed' for the murder as his adulterous relationship had ended years before. Within a month Domingo was acquitted and, since Pedro was never found, there the case ended.

For both Marie and María, their actions had led to extreme responses from their husbands. Their affairs had caused turmoil and scandal in their communities. For both, the consequences of adultery were catastrophic. One was killed by her dishonoured husband and the other was abandoned by family and state to a slow death in a dungeon. In their individual way, both of these cases move the discussion of adultery and its relationship to familial and especially male honour to the strident responses societies from the Renaissance to the Enlightenment had to female adultery as opposed to male adultery.

The 1650 English Adultery Act made the distinction clear. A married woman who had sex with someone other than her husband, or a single woman who had sex with a married man were committing adultery for which the official punishment was death. A man in a similar situation was guilty of 'fornication' and liable to a lesser punishment. No wonder then that women were advised in the *Court of Good Counsell* (1607) that 'a woman should take heede, that she give not man occasion to thinke hardly of her, either by her Deedes, Wordes, Lookes or Apparell'. As we have noted, the threat posed by female adultery to paternity, inheritance, and familial honour or reputation made this double standard almost inescapable.

Four cases from sixteenth century Geneva show how this legal double standard could work in practice. In 1558, Jean Gosse and Marie Villiers, both from Champagne, were arrested. They had lived together as man and wife in Lyon where they had converted to Protestantism. Jean had taken Marie there to get her away from her husband who was a mercenary and had been forcing her to prostitute herself. Once they had converted and arrived in Geneva they had confessed their irregular arrangement to Nicolas Colladon, one of the city's ministers (and brother to the city's chief legal advisor). Jean was condemned for fornication and perpetually banished. However, Marie was deemed guilty of multiple adulteries and was flogged through the streets 'until her blood flowed' and then banished as well.

Over a decade later, in 1570, Dominique Buisard and Clauda Mermod were arrested for adultery. Clauda had married eight years before but had left her husband and come to Geneva four years previous to the trial. She had had 'imprudent contact tending to fornication' with a number of her employer's male servants and had been jailed for her behaviour. Later, while working at an inn, her husband had come and begged her to return to him but she had refused. Soon thereafter, she had exchanged promises with another man and, a fortnight later, she and a third man were caught by her mistress in a garden owned by the innkeeper. The two officers who had followed them with the innkeeper's wife had broken down the door and found them *in flagrante*, had taken Dominique's sword and dagger and placed them under arrest.

Dominque said that he was simply passing through Geneva and had met Clauda. He had solicited her, despite having his own spouse in Lausanne. He claimed he did know that she was married – though he certainly was aware of his own marital status. They had groped and he had 'polluted himself but not in her'. She claimed that she had deserted her husband because 'they could not have sex [because he was impotent] and he had given her permission to see if she could... change her fortune'. The husband admitted that they had not had sex but could give no real explanation for their failure to consummate the marriage.

Two legal opinions survive. In one, the lawyer accepted that Dominique was ignorant of Marie's marital status and should, therefore, be spared execution. Marie, since her marriage had never been consummated, was not really married (quite correctly, under Canon Law). Her lewd behaviour otherwise merited a flogging. Colladon's opinion takes a different approach. Her actions tended to fornication in every sense and she may have been prostituting herself (her status as a servant at an inn may be informing his view) and Dominique knew he was married. They should both be executed. The state split the difference in the socially acceptable manner: he was flogged and banished; she was drowned.

What is interesting though is that the dossier contains extracts from the city's various edicts giving the permutations of adultery and the recommended punishments:

DEFENDANT	PUNISHMENT
Married man *with*	12 days in jail and 3 hours in the stock
single female *or*	12 days in jail and a fine
single female servant	Banished on pain of death
Married woman *with*	Executed
Single male *or*	Flogged and banished
Single male servant	Executed
Married man *with*	Executed
Married female	Executed

Nothing could make the double standard more apparent. However, one should note closely that a female domestic servant was punished much less harshly than a male domestic. The obvious explanation is that the male domestic had actually 'robbed' his master both of his honour and his wife's chastity. The socio-cultural crime was the adultery of the married woman. Even the relatively lenient sentence against the single (non-servant) male supports the view. He may have damaged the husband but it was not an affront to his master. This view was widely held across Europe. English ecclesiastical courts were relatively tolerant of married men's adulteries *unless* they took place with a female domestic; such lewdness should be kept out of the home. The *Athenian Mercury* (1691) which we have already encountered proposing affection in marriage also supported this general double standard (perhaps sarcastically) when it said, 'some indeed think [women] have *Learn'd* enough, if they can distinguish between their *Husbands Breeches* and another *mans*'.

The subjugation and subservience expected of women was almost inconceivable. William Gouge in his manual for wives (*Of Domesticall Duties*) in the third treatise 'on a wife's one particular and peculiar duty' (i.e., subjection) noted that a wife could, with propriety, call her husband 'Lord', 'Husband' or 'Master + Surname'. But never 'Brother', 'Friend', 'Sweet', 'Love' or, worse, by his Christian/first name. A husband might call his wife 'Wife', 'Love' or 'Dove' but never 'Lady', 'Mistress', 'Dame' or 'Mother' as these could be construed to imply equality. The level of learning advised for a good wife, satyrised by the *Athenian Mercury*, was supported implicitly by John Winthrop in his journal when he noted that the wife of Governor Hopkins of Connecticut went mad because:

> of her giving herself wholly to reading and writing… For if she had attended her household duties and such things as belong to women, and not gone out of her way and calling to meddle in such things as are proper to men, whose minds are stronger… she had [*sic*] kept her wits.

Despite this obvious double standard, men could not count on escaping the harsher penalties for adultery every time. In 1561, Jacques le Nepveu was beheaded in Geneva for multiple adulterous relationships. He himself was not married and though he had importuned his master's wife they had not had sex. His sentence appears to have been death because of the frequency of his sins. However, the state did accept his appeal that his body be buried rather than being exhibited on the gibbet – the fate of his head is not known.

In the case of Henri Philippe, his assumptions about the attitudes of his fellow male citizens was greatly mistaken. He was prosecuted in 1560 for 'adultery and a dissolute life'. He had been seen on numerous occasions, in public, trying to seduce (and solicit with money) a newlywed, Nicolarde Bastard, who had been a servant in his family's home. Another former servant, Clauda Barrachin, told a similar tale. An extract from the Consistory's records tells of his adultery (he had been married for twenty years) with Nicolarde and a third servant, named Pernette and his importuning of Berthe (wife of Jean Dexert). He also admitted to possessing a 'figure graven on glass' (a magic charm) made for him by a carpenter in Lausanne.

The legal advice (by Colladon, Spifame and Dorsanne) said that his various crimes (perjury, adultery, possessing a charm) were such that although 'heretofore, in this city, one has not punished [male] adulterers by capital punishment in keeping with the Divine and civil laws', he should be executed. Despite this strong advice, the court (and Senate) decided he should be flogged through the streets until he was bloodied. Unwilling to have himself humiliated and with the active support of his wife, Jeanne, he appealed (as was his right as a native-born citizen) to the larger Genevan Council of Two Hundred. The appeal went disastrously wrong as the council announced itself unhappy with the trial records and demanded further investigations. They also took additional legal advice from the three lawyers who said, 'it seems, in keeping with the previous advice, that he justly merits the death penalty ordained by Divine law and the constitutions of Christian emperors'. The council eventually overturned the decision of the court and Senate and sentenced him to be decapitated and exposed on the gibbet.

The council could, on occasion, be more lenient though. In 1560, Claude Clerc (his wife will feature below in an adultery case of 1570) turned himself in for adultery with Pernette de Ulmoz in a stable six months before. His conscience had got the better of him. He used this as an occasion to confess to a fight with a French teenager (aged about fourteen) and some fornication a decade before. For his previous sexual crimes he had been jailed for six days and been given a small fine. He had subsequently married (about five years later) and had now committed adultery. The court sentenced him to a public flogging but the Council of Two Hundred reduced this to nine days in jail and a larger fine (25 florins instead of the previous 5 florins).

These cases serve to remind us of the impact of the double standard as well as its limitations. As we have already noted, the point at which most men found their beneficial position limited was at their own front doors. Even though the Genevan model, outlined above, makes clear that a master's involvement with a domestic servant was theoretically to be punished less harshly, the reality (as in England) was different. However, the cases that follow will make the point that Geneva took a much less severe view of adultery than their laws implied and, in particular, on a case-by-case basis they made decisions which often seem impossible to understand or explain. The result, though, was often leniency for women.

In 1558, Robert le Crosnier, a journeyman printer working for the famous printer and martyologist, Jean Crespin, was prosecuted for adultery with Jeanne, wife of Mathieu Vernel.

Two men, Claude Chiccand and Mathieu Michard, had watched at a keyhole and caught the pair *in flagrante*. They had not completely consummated the relationship but they both confessed that 'they had fornicated a little bit together and had kissed one another and fondled one another'. Although the Genevan model suggested execution for Jeanne (as a married woman) and a flogging and banishment for Robert (and perhaps execution, as he was a servant) they were both jailed for nine days and banished on pain of being flogged. That is, their punishment was much more that of a married man and a single (non-domestic) female.

Another case from 1558 also led to a lenient sentence. Vincent Masson adulterated with the wife of his master, Gilles le Lievre (printer), on a number of occasions. Moreover, it was clear that the wife, Jeanne, was trying to convince Vincent to take her away from Geneva. She told the court that she wanted to live in some other Protestant place because her husband 'was too mean'. Vincent said he had been seduced by Satan into the affair. The court decided that they had given in to 'their evil desire, affection, and carnal concupiscence' and that leaving town was simply a way to ensure they could continue in 'the abominable act of adultery'. He was beaten through the city and banished; no record survives of her sentence. If one supposes she was jailed and fined then their punishment was that suggested for a married master and his female domestic.

A similar leniency operated in the case (1562) of Judith Tournent (wife of Leonard du Mazel) and her lover, Etienne Gemeau (her husband's employee). After close and intense questioning they both admitted that they had had sex at least four times including once when her husband was 'having supper *chez* Mon. Calvin'. He also admitted to a number of fornications with 'the sort of abandoned women one finds in the countryside'. It was also revealed that Judith had been 'instructed in the faith of God [i.e., Protestantism] from her youth' and that she had been repeatedly admonished by her husband and others for her drinking. Despite this catalogue of sins, they were both flogged through the city and banished on pain of death.

Lest one conclude that Geneva was a bastion of leniency one must consider the case of Catherine de Courtarval (of a very noble Maine family), wife of a hero of the Genevan Revolution, François Bonivard (made famous in Byron's *The Prisoner of Chillon*) with his servant, Claude Fatton. She was drowned for her adultery and he was beheaded. Though this sentence was very much in line with the Genevan theory it actually masks a complex case which implies the severity had more to do with their backgrounds and previous sexual histories than the actual adultery case before the court.

Catherine was a former 'nun in a Papist convent' who had removed herself from 'under the shadow' to live 'in the great liberty and purity of conscience under the holy reformation of the Gospel [in Geneva]'. Then she had entered into a private marriage with a man and had a child. Having committed this sin, she left Geneva to return to the convent 'to pollute [the same term used for sexual defilement and ejaculation] herself in Papist abominations'. Again she abandoned the religious life and committed adultery with a man in Tours and had another child. Returning to Geneva she was hauled before the Consistory, admonished, handed over to the secular arm, and banished. After entreaties, she was allowed to return to the city. She then married Bonivard (a former prior and, thus, presumably sympathetic to Catherine's plight) who was over sixty and 'impotent in his members'. She abused his kindness and wasted his money. The relationship with Claude began and they had had sex repeatedly and were not particularly circumspect in their behaviour. She had found him an apprenticeship (the court noted his youth) and nine letters were found promising marriage should Bonivard die. She also said that she had once been married briefly to Robert Gradin who had died in Lausanne and her one legitimate son had died unbaptised after living a few days. Finally, she said her father was a servant of 'Mon. d'Alençon, first husband of the Queen of Navarre'.

Claude's background was less spectacular but also troubling to the court. He was the bastard son of a Burgundian priest. He had been an Augustinian monk and priest in his home village where he had committed fornication with some of his parishioners. He had stolen 20 francs from his monastery (where he was factor) and defrauded his aunt of another sixteen (saying he was off to study letters in Paris) to allow him and a friend to come to Geneva. He also confessed that they had begun a slander suit against a chambermaid, Barbe le Bois, to discredit any accusations she might make against them.

All of these confessions make the case considerably more complex and shocking than a simple case of adultery between a male servant and his master's wife. Their rather dubious adherence to Protestantism, their repeated sexual adventures, the theft, the scandal, all combined to convince the court that an exemplary punishment was required. Finally, the confession that Claude had regularly shaved Catherine's genitals left the court stunned. When asked, Catherine said she had learned this behaviour 'at the convent'. Perhaps unsuprisingly, she was drowned and he was beheaded with his body exposed on the gibbet and his head nailed nearby.

Finally, as with sex before marriage, the mere appearance of impropriety or over-familiarity with a member of the opposite sex could cause scandal and precipitate a case. Pierre Bouloz, a poor labourer, and his wife Thevena Jaccod were arrested, in 1562, for allowing another worker to share their bed one night at a construction site at the rural château of Mon. Lullin (a leading politician). Originally, the husband had been in the middle but both he and his wife had got up in the night 'to pass water' and the sleeping arrangements had become disordered and the young man had ended up next to Thevena. The couple were banished for this indiscretion.

Nor was such treatment reserved for poor labourers. Pierre du Perril, the head of Geneva's general hospital, was prosecuted for over-familiarity with Georgea Martin, the wife of Claude Clerc (a citizen butcher – and confessed adulterer, see above). Both admitted that they had known one another since they were children. They often spoke and socialised in each other's homes. When asked 'if she knew it was prohibited for "quality" to carry on this way and if she had ever been admonished she replied he was not above her station'. Georgea admitted that Pierre's wife (Elizabeth Pathey) had once called her 'such a whore' in the street but she had responded by saying 'she was as good a woman as she was'. They were made to apologise in public and sent to the Consistory for admonition. In addition, he was sacked from his civic post and told that if he ever went to her house again he would be arrested and convicted of adultery no matter what had actually happened.

What one realises from these cases taken together is that theory and practice often varied dramatically. The cases have been selected for a reason. They come from a place, Geneva, and a period, Calvin's ascendancy there, noted across Europe in the sixteenth century for its enthusiastic religious environment and rigorous application of high moral standards. Even here, though, the simple view of adultery as a serious crime for which women were punished harshly and sex with domestic servants even more so can be seen to be too simplistic. In most cases, in Geneva and elsewhere, the application of justice was much more *ad hoc* and 'situational'. That is, the particular circumstances of the adulterous relationship, the previous sexual histories of the defendants, their religious views, their socio-economic and political status, their ages and their occupations were all factored into a complex equation which produced a verdict. Justice was more than the mere application of laws and moral theories. If was often a negotiation involving judges, defendants, the various factors just mentioned, and the wider community. More often than not, the law (strictly speaking) and religious opinions had a much less significant role.

One final type of adultery must be considered before moving to a conclusion. Bigamy was, by its definition, adulterous but it also contained an element of premeditation and perjury that made it particularly offensive to early modern societies. Moreover, it struck at the heart not only of individual and familial honour but also the reputation of the wider community. Especially after the Reformation, there were two charges no society would want levelled against it by its opponents: the toleration of polygamy or the religious views that were normally associated with multiple marriages – Anabaptism.

Conrad Ricaud and Madeleine Cavin were arrested in 1561 for bigamy. She admitted freely that she had become engaged to Conrad while her first and late husband (Jean Preudhomme) was still alive. Conrad had initially asked to marry her young daughter but when she had refused he had proposed to her. They both admitted that they had had sex once before coming to Geneva. Conrad had suggested that they move to the city (whence he had been previously banished and then re-admitted for suspicion of adultery) so that 'the magistrates could divorce her from her husband who is of an evil life'. She had believed this 'being badly advised and badly taught'. He had assumed the divorce would be granted, after the fact, since the man was now dead and had been 'a fornicator and dissolute'. Their crime then would have been no more than one act of 'anticipation'. Colladon thought these excuses no more than that and advised that they be flogged and banished on pain of another flogging; the sentence was duly applied.

The case (also in 1561) against the citizen Claude Plantain and a couple (Maurice Gaillard and his wife, Françoise Pommière) was bizarre. Claude was arrested for being engaged to two sisters at the same time. The Gaillards had known of the arrangement and were also prosecuted. The two sisters were the wards of the Gaillards and the younger sisters of Françoise. Claude had been offered the elder sister (Clauda) but had said he preferred the younger sister (Jannaz). Clauda, he told them, 'is too fat and too old'. The judges banished all of them on pain of being flogged.

Two years previously (1559), Charles Fournaut had tried to use the Protestant view on divorce in his defence. He was arrested for adultery and (intent to) bigamy. He had come to Geneva having converted to Protestantism and become engaged to Thomasse de Reancourt, a domestic servant. A number of other religious refugees from his hometown of Rouen testified that he was already married and his wife was still alive. However, he argued that she had committed adultery four years before and 'had ruptured the oath of marriage and had given him a serious illness [i.e., a venereal disease]'. The judges accepted his version of the events and noted, in particular, the fervency of his conversion ('about which he had sworn solemnly'). Nevertheless, he was publicly humiliated, paraded through the streets carrying a torch and banished on pain of being flogged. This case gives some idea of how difficult it was to escape one's past. As many of the other cases have shown, in an age when mobility might be unexpected, the reality was that one was almost inevitably going to encounter a 'neighbour' wherever one went.

Humbert Maniglier, in 1558, had also tried to argue that the adultery of his first wife had broken the marriage. However, when he was confronted with a letter from the Consistory in the Bernese-controlled village of Moudon he had had to admit that he had 'not obtained any divorce from the court or the Consistory'. The authorities from Moudon, in subsequent letters, refuted his accusations and said his first wife was 'a woman of good repute and honour' who had lived 'honestly and without scandal' since being abandoned by Maniglier. What is interesting in comparing this case (of clear abandonment) and that of Fournaut (whose wife was an adulterer) is that the punishment was almost identical. Maniglier was also humiliated in public, paraded through the streets (with a mitre on his head rather than bearing a torch) and then banished (though on pain of death). In practical terms the punishments were the same.

Although an appeal to Protestant beliefs about divorce was not successful, there was always the possibility of using the traditional views on 'private marriages'. In 1566, Clauda Simon was prosecuted for being engaged to two men (François Mercier, a licentiate in law, and Jean-Baptiste Payari, a merchant from Cremona). Both men were of some social standing. Clauda admitted that she had exchanged tokens and promises with Mercier in front of witnesses. However, she had been concerned that he might not have parental permission and argued that the entire arrangement was conditional (a promise of future marriage). Her mother (Jeanne le Piccard, widow of Jacques Simon), an aunt (Anne Perrin, wife of Antoine Bertholet), Jehanton du Bois, and Bartholomy Joural had witnessed the arrangement including the discussion of bride-price and dowry. They all agreed though that the agreement was, in part, conditional. By the time Mercier had obtained parental permission, Clauda had become engaged to Payari, the Italian merchant.

Colladon attempted to sort out this complex situation in keeping with the efforts of the clergy and bureaucrats to bring marriage under the control of church and state. He argued that the first promise was entirely conditional and, since the city's ordinances did not recognise conditional promises, they were wholly invalid. By the time they were valid the second set of negotiations was underway. Thus, the discussions and promises with Payeri were the only ones that were valid. Clauda should be chastised, not for the complexity of her dealings, but for having any further contact with Mercier. Also, she should be made to declare before the Consistory that her dealings with Mercier were wholly invalid and that she was, in fact, going to marry Payeri. In addition to accepting this advice, the court also jailed her for three days.

These lenient sentences belie the potential of the law. In 1567, Bastian de la Costa (from Genoa) was arrested for bigamy. Despite his efforts to claim that his first wife had been 'a whore' and had died or 'so he had heard', the court discovered that she was very much alive and was an honest woman whom he had abandoned, along with their daughter, without reason. After working in Milan, Strasbourg and Basle (one notes again the mobility of an individual) he settled in Zurich. There he had repeatedly importuned a young girl. Nine months before his trial he had moved to Geneva attracted, so he said, by the Italian church there. Three months after his arrival he had married 'an honest and virtuous woman, a widow'. He had seen people who knew him from Genoa and Zurich. They were able to attest to his dissolute life and pre-existing marriage. To avoid being recognised he had tried to move his household from their rooms near the cathedral (in the centre of town) to St-Gervaise (the suburb across the river). In addition, he had twice tried to break out of jail as he knew 'that bigamy was punished by death in Geneva though it only merited a term in the galleys in Genoa'. For his general infamy and gross deceit of his Genevan wife, Hilaire (who pleaded for his life before the court), he was beheaded.

It would be a mistake to assume that even the legal theories were accepted without question. Not only was the practice of the courts in dealing with adultery and other sexual crimes between men and women more complex than the law might imply, but there were voices that argued for an altogether different approach. For example, as early as the sixteenth century, Montaigne was arguing that 'custom' was a harmful restraint on the pursuit of 'pure knowledge and pleasure'. Even earlier, utopian writings in the late Renaissance had envisioned societies where men and women were concerned with love and innocence not 'honour'. Honour was seen as the artificial and culturally constructed product of custom and opinion; it was, in fact, a tyrant.

By the end of our period, Enlightenment thinkers were adding another layer to the discussion. With the move to marriage based on affection (real emotional attachment), there was an increasing stress on the couple as a unit. For many, this was primarily an economic unit which played an integral part in the wider society and its advances and stability. In particular, late eighteenth-century economists argued the punishment of adultery and fornication was not primarily predicated on godliness but the need to support (legitimate) population growth since this increase was an essential part of economic expansion and the increase of wealth. Marriage, especially monogamy, was to be promoted because celibate women and prostitutes were not 'efficient breeders'. Prostitutes were especially inefficient because they could have sex with ten men but not produce ten children. Interestingly, they never came to the conclusion that polygamy (one man impregnating two or more women) would produce an even greater increase.

Thus the late eighteenth century, in addition to producing new images of gender and sex, also found a new basis for sustaining, through strict laws, the sexual *status quo*. Hence, Adam Smith, that great exponent of *laissez-faire* freedom in business, said of female adultery that:

> [a] breach of chastity dishonours irretrievably. No circumstances, no solicitation, can excuse it; no sorrow, no

repentance atone for it. We are so nice in this respect, that even a rape dishonours, and the innocence of the [victim's] mind cannot, in our imaginations wash out the pollution of the body.

Robert Malthus added to the burden on women and buttressed traditional religious arguments with demography by arguing that any form of contraception, since it inhibited the population's increase, was an 'improper act'. Writers went so far as to suggest the frequency of sex in marriage. Daniel Rogers, in *Matrimonial Honour* (1642), had suggested that once a week was appropriate. Combined with the Protestant rejection of abstinence in marriage for devotional reasons, the rejection of contraceptives, and the newly promoted ideas of economics coupled with pre-existing religious beliefs, the Enlightenment hardly proved to be a liberating experience for women for all it stressed freedom and individual liberty.

Even where voices echoing Montaigne's opposition to custom were heard they exposed ideas which, today, still sound fairly phallo-centric. Thus, when Bentham said that sodomy was better than prostitution or masturbation and that England's sodomy laws of the late eighteenth century reminded one of the Spanish Inquisition, he was certainly not advocating female sexual liberation. Instead, it is wholly appropriate to end this chapter with some quotations that emphasise the enduring stress laid on female chastity.

In 1792, an anonymous tract, *The Evils of Adultery and Prostitution*, said 'the increasing debauchery of the present age, and [the] avowal of adultery and every kind of licentiousness, introduce a general corruption of manners'. John Blunt, *Man-Midwifery Dissected* (1793), laid the blame squarely on the too frequent mixing of the sexes outside of marriage and, in particular, in gynecology: 'it is the almost universal custom of employing men-midwives, [to which] I attribute the frequent adulteries which disgrace our country'. Adam Sibbit (1799) was just as convinced that the loosening of the marital bonds was having a disastrous impact on the nation:

> Among the various instances of moral depravity which too clearly indicate the corruption of the age in which we live, the frequency of divorces [is a] feature of degeneracy which at present [gives] the greatest alarm… The crime of adultery seems to prevail to such a degree, as to threaten the very existence of society.

We can be sure that he did not mean the adulteries of men. Female chastity remained the issue and explains why he said a year later: 'the manners of women, in every state, have always arrived at their climax of corruption immediately preceding [the state's] destruction'.

three

PROSTITUTES
AND THE PERVERSION
OF SEX FOR PROFIT

O ne might easily believe that recent attitudes to prostitution have been around almost as long as the profession itself. Christian morals seem so clear on many aspects of
sexuality that there must never have been any differing
approach to prostitution. Surely, societies from the
Renaissance to the Enlightenment were constant and consistent in pursuing and prosecuting both prostitutes and their
clients. In fact, this is most certainly not the case. Specific
aspects of early modern culture made prostitution necessary
if not attractive to many ruling authorities. In contrast, various
religious movements (for example, the Reformation and
Catholic religious orders) were strongly opposed to any toleration of the behaviour.

Late medieval and early modern societies faced a number
of problems. Most importantly, the system of training for
skilled workers was based on the apprentice, journeyman and
master system. A labourer began to train for a skill in his local

community under the tutelage of a master. For the most part, these apprentices actually lived in the home, shop and out-buildings of the master and his family (which normally included female domestic servants and daughters). It was rela-tively easy to keep apprentices in line since they could be dismissed and their desire to avoid shame to their wider fami-lies served as a check on behaviour. The greatest sexual threat posed by apprentices was either sex with one another in the multiple-occupancy beds and rooms, or sex with domestics and younger females in the household.

At the second stage of a worker's education, he became a journeyman. As such he was required to leave his homeland and spend time working under a number of masters in other locales. Again, some journeymen lived with their masters. However, journeymen were very different from apprentices. Most apprentices were in their late teens while journeymen were 'twenty-somethings'. Also, many journeymen were housed in large dormitory buildings run by the guild or trade for which they were training. Quite often they organised themselves into 'young men's societies' (called *Abbeys* in French-speaking countries). In reality, these were little more than gangs.

Late medieval and early modern societies had a great deal of trouble controlling the behaviour of these societies. They caroused, drank and brawled endlessly. Also, they were over-loaded with testosterone and sexual desire. There was a very real fear that these young men would gang-rape 'respectable' women and especially maidens in the streets − nor, as many records attest, was the fear an idle one. Likewise, they were even more concerned about the possibility that journeymen (living alone in dormitories) might be more likely to turn to one another (sodomy) than apprentices (who lived under the watchful eyes of their masters and families). The legal inability of journeymen to marry before becoming masters meant that these threats often continued and grew as, in practice, this meant single men could not really hope to marry until their early thirties.

For all these reasons, prostitutes seemed the ideal answer to the problem. Respectable women's virtue was protected, male sexual aggression was released, and the men's sexuality channeled into 'appropriate' (i.e., heterosexual) avenues rather than into sodomitical habits. As late as 1796, William Buchan, in his *Observations Concerning the Prevention and Cure of the Venereal Disease*, said that the elimination of prostitution would simply drive men into one another's arms. Consequently, most cities and towns in the late fifteenth and early sixteenth centuries either tolerated or actually provided brothels for 'the public good'. In addition to alleviating the problem posed by journeymen these prostitutes also provided an acceptable outlet for the sexual adventures of married men, providing sexual release without any serious threat to the family unit (as a socio-economic building-block of society). Indeed, a town like Dijon (in the Renaissance) built a large building (brothel) with multiple bedrooms each provided with a stone fireplace for the use of the prostitutes and their clients.

However, this tolerant – or, rather, pragmatic – approach was not without its critics. Many Catholic religious orders, in particular the Franciscans, before the Reformation attacked this obvious sexual decadence. Even they, though, were often more concerned about the implicit toleration of sodomy amongst the unmarried and between men and adolescent youths. With the Reformation, the attack on lax sexuality only grew though, again, the focus was not necessarily on prostitution. Most Reformers were initially more concerned about the sexuality of the supposedly celibate priests, monks and nuns of the old church. However, as they resolved this by elevating the role of marriage, they also stressed the need to transform former brothel workers into 'respectable' wives and mothers. Some German Protestant towns offered financial incentives to men willing to marry 'reformed' prostitutes.

The assault on prostitution by religious authorities was not, by itself, especially successful. Protestantism and, eventually, Counter-Reformation Catholicism closed most brothels or forced them underground. Women who had worked and been given a modicum of comfort and protection in brothels were driven into the streets or separately rented rooms where they were considerably more vulnerable to extortion and abuse. To eliminate prostitution, a method was needed to convince individual men to avoid prostitutes.

Medical science provided an answer, albeit not a completely successful one. In the late 1490s, Western Europe was beset by a new and loathsome disease – venereal disease (most commonly, though not necessarily convincingly, equated with modern syphilis). Unlike modern venereal diseases, in its initial form, this disease disfigured and killed its victims quickly. The cankers and running sores were appalling and the normally prescribed treatments (dosing with mercury) almost as lethal. Although it is true that early modern medicine was woefully inadequate for the challenges it faced, it was able to identify this disease with sexual activity. Almost immediately, the new disease was attached to illicit sexual activity and societies responded appropriately. In 1546, Henry VIII ordered the closure of all bathhouses (the Stews) to which many streetwalkers had repaired to ply their trades after the suppression of the brothels. By 1560 and the advent of the Reformation in Scotland, Scottish edicts were ordering the expulsion of all prostitutes from the realm.

Many of these reactions parallel initial responses to HIV/AIDS (for example, the immediate closure of San Francisco's saunas). In addition, although associated with sexual activity, there was a widespread belief that venereal disease could be passed (again, as with general beliefs about HIV/AIDS) by drinking vessels, utensils, sheets, clothing and lavatories. Medical practitioners supported this belief. It certainly seems to have been the case that the disease could be spread to infants through breast-feeding. This meant that two groups could be seen – and targeted – uniquely as focal points for the spread of the disease: prostitutes and wet-nurses. It is hardly surprising, therefore, to see that this was used in the on-going moral campaigns against prostitution and wet-nursing. Ministers and moralists were given an invaluable weapon in their armoury against these groups.

There was more to this, though, than simply seeing prostitutes and wet-nurses as conduits for the disease. They were the *source* of the illness. Women, diseased women, passed the illness to male *victims*. One story, dating from the 1630s but widely repeated well into the 1800s (and given impetus and prominence by John Marten's influential work on venereal disease in 1708), makes this point. Thomas Johnston's translation of Ambroise Paré's magisterial work on medicine told that a man had given in to his wife's demands for a wet-nurse to help her as she was short of milk. He took in a woman who seemed, externally, to be morally upright. Sadly, she was diseased. While nursing, she passed the illness to the infant who then infected his own mother when she was able to nurse. Through sex, the woman then gave her husband the disease and he later infected his two other small children with whom he often shared a bed (and, thus, the sheets). Through indulging his wife and engaging in a practice (wet-nursing) widely condemned by ministers and moralists (as unmaternal) and medical authorities (as dangerous) the family was destroyed.

Any place to which 'lewd women' resorted could now be labelled as a cesspit of infection. William Cowes, writing in 1596, said, 'it is wonderfull to consider how huge multitudes there be of such as be infect… [in] lewd alehouses' and these places were 'the very nests and haborers of such filthy [i.e., diseased] creatures'. The threat of the disease could also be used by some for polemical as well as moralising purposes. For example, Protestant writers and preachers often warned their followers of the dangers of 'celibate' Catholics who used the confessional as an easy place to debauch women and, as a result, spread disease. The 1680 anonymous tract, *The Whore of Babylon's Pockey Priest*, is but one example among many.

Nevertheless, this might still leave some readers thinking that these women were no more than the means by which the disease spread. However, medical authorities understood the situation very differently. First of all, this was a disease passed by illicit sex. A chaste, married woman could not infect her husband (*pace* the nursing woman who had indulged in the practice of wet-nursing and suffered accordingly). David Sennert, a leading medical authority, wrote (in 1673): 'truly men contact this evil from women that are infected, because in the [sex] act… the Womb being heated, vapors are raised from the malignant humours in the womb, which are suck't in by the man's Yard'. A similar explanation was advanced by Thomas Needham (1700): 'the Pocky Steams of the diseased woman do often evidently imprint their malignity on the genitals of the healthy play-fellows [i.e., men]'. Needham's comment wonderfully encapsulated the view. The (loose) woman, or prostitute, was diseased while the man was merely the harmless-sounding 'play-fellow'. An alternative view was expressed by Gideon Harvey (in 1672) who argued that most prostitutes were 'frigid'; that is, they were not aroused (because of their disinterest) by the sex act. Their wombs did not, therefore, become 'hot' enough to enliven the disease. However, even he warned that a handsome man might be in danger if the prostitute became aroused during the sex act.

Just as these men were writing, though, the medical world was being introduced to another theory of the disease which completely identified the epidemic with loose morals, in general, and loose women in particular. Nicolas de Blegny, whose work was translated into English in 1670 by Walter Harris and popularised in 1684 in *A New Method of Curing the French Pox*, made significant refinements on the prevailing theories. Since women were normally seen as humourally 'cold' there were serious problems with the 'heated womb' theory. Also, the increasing popularity of chemical approaches to medicine (epitomised by the use of mercurial doses to treat venereal disease) meant a new theory was needed.

In de Blegny's view the disease was actually produced in the wombs of loose women. As a result of sex with various men their wombs were the repositories of the semen of a number of men. This semen was retained where, mixing together, it rotted and fermented, encouraged by the heat of the woman's womb. This 'adulteration' of semen – the moral and chemical connotations of the word were obvious – resulted in a new and noxious compound: venereal disease. Any man placing his member in so diseased a vessel (the womb) and applying heat (sex) was bound to become infected. The surest defence, therefore, was fidelity in marriage or chastity, depending on one's marital state.

These medical theories, accompanied by a wider attack on loose morals by ministers and reformers, produced a view of prostitution which increasingly made it sound like sodomy. A few examples will suffice to make this point. In 1714, Richard Boulton wrote that 'when... a woman [has sex] with different persons, the *course of nature is perverted* and the semen [ferments into pox]'. Later in the century (1776) during a sermon to the 'reformed' prostitutes and beneficiaries of the Magdalen Hospital in London, William Dodd, chaplain, said, 'every man who reflects on the true condition of humanity, must know that the life of a common prostitute is as *contrary to the nature* and condition of the female sex as darkness is to light'. Although the emphases are mine, the language is moving very close to that used for sodomy as a 'crime against nature'. Finally, in early eighteenth-century London, effeminate males who frequently lived and dressed as women were increasingly referred to as 'mollies', a slang term originally meaning 'whore'.

While these were the theories about, and responses to, prostitution, it is essential that actual trials of prostitutes and 'lewd' women be examined. Again, because of its exceptional criminal court records for the whole of the period from the Renaissance to the Enlightenment, Geneva provides an outstanding cache of cases relating to prostitution. One of the most spectacular occurred in 1566, just two years after Calvin's death and under the ministry of Beza.

In March, Louise Maistre was arrested for multiple adultery and fornication. She came from a troubled background which seems to have driven her into prostitution. Her first husband, Jean-Jacques Bonivard, was the publican of the Green Dog tavern and a baker. In 1550, he and Louise had been hauled before the Consistory and the courts for 'keeping a disorderly house' which in Geneva meant domestic discord including, as in this case, physical violence against Louise. In 1558, she and others were arrested for consorting with Calvin's exiled political opponents. Her second husband, Jean-François Cugnard, also had a troubled history. In 1546, he had been arrested for public brawling but was released because of his youth (i.e., he was probably a teenager). He was also associated with Calvin's political opponents. In the months and years after Louise's execution (December 1566, 1569 and 1571) he was arrested for theft and a 'dissolute life'. Taken together, these other trials testify to Louise's life of poverty and violent circumstances.

Her clients were many and much is known of them. Indeed, this case gives an interesting insight into the 'underbelly' of early modern Genevan society at the height of Calvinist 'morality' in the city. Guillaume de la Fin confessed that he had had sex with her ten to twelve years before when she had come to him to buy some wine. She said she had no money but suggested that 'if he would value something else and had not had a woman' she could suggest an alternative form of payment. He agreed and they had done the same the next day but he said never thereafter, as she had also testified. Two years before, Guillaume was jailed for beating his wife and allowing his daughter's suitor to lodge with the family. A year after Louise's trial he was punished for slandering a leading Genevan merchant, François de Chasteauneuf, and charging excessive interest on a large loan – implying he may have consorted with the poor but was not himself without means.

Her second paramour, Charles Goulaz, was the citizen son of a prominent magistrate. He admitted that he had previously been punished by the courts for fathering a bastard child (though not by Louise). For consorting with Louise he was fined and jailed 'on bread and water' for six days (as Guillaume de la Fin had been). A few years before Louise's trial, Goulaz and others had been prosecuted for dancing at a wedding. François Clerc, another citizen, received a similar fine but got nine days in jail for his relations with Louise eighteen years before. His record seems otherwise spotless and one can only assume that his greater punishment was because he had hidden the crime for so many years.

Jean Losserand, the elder, a naturalised citizen, admitted that he had had sex with Louise twice about thirteen years before after his wife had died, and had given her some money afterwards. Louise was, he had to admit, married at the time so technically this was adultery. For this crime, he also got six days in jail and a small fine. Later that same year, he was placed in the stocks for two hours for perjury in an incest case involving Jean Rivet and his sister-in-law. Jehanton du Bois, a citizen and soldier admitted that, as with many of the others, he had had sex with Louise about fifteen years before, once at his house and once *chez* Louise. They were both married and he 'is greatly repentant'. His small fine and nine days in jail seems paltry when one considers his past record. In 1542 he had been prosecuted for denying that Geneva had any authority over him since he had signed up to a mercenary company and was, therefore, only answerable to his captain. More germane to this case, in 1553 he had fathered a child in fornication.

Jacques de Lonnex, another citizen, said he had slept with Louise fourteen years previously when 'she held the Green Dog'. Indeed, it seems that she was single-handedly running a brothel on the side of her husband's inn. With or without his knowledge is not known though it may explain their marital discord – or have caused it. For his relations with Louise, Jacques was also jailed for six days and fined. He was also prosecuted four times from 1559 to 1567 for contact with Calvin's political opponents. The close connection of many of her clients and herself with Calvin's defeated opponents might imply that the inn served as the meeting-place for this Genevan political faction.

Another of her paramours, Guillaume Messeri (of another prominent citizen family) also confessed to having had sex with her eighteen years before 'when she held the tavern'. He had been single at the time though, clearly, she was married. He was fined and jailed for six days. In the period immediately before the trial (1559–62) he was prosecuted on three separate occasions: for contact with Calvin's exiled opponents; for dancing (with Goulaz, see above); for buying property from (i.e., swindling) a minor without the permission of his guardian. Two final clients both confessed to sex with Louise twelve years before. Jean Saultier, citizen, was jailed for six days and fined. He was otherwise unknown to the courts. Claude Blanchet, citizen, was not so anonymous. In addition to being jailed for six days and fined for sex with Louise, in 1551 and 1557 he had been prosecuted for fornication with two other women.

This rather extensive discussion of a single case serves to highlight the hypocrisy of even a supposedly moral city, Calvinist Geneva. At the very moment that Knox was holding Geneva up as that most Christian of cities ever, the city's fathers were fining and jailing for a few days prominent figures (many of whom would later hold high office). On the other hand, Louise was drowned for adultery. And yet, in every sense of the word, all these men were also adulterers. As we have seen in an earlier chapter, the 'adultery' of a man was mere fornication because it had no impact on paternity or inheritance within the family. Moreover, sex with a 'lewd' woman or prostitute was of even less importance and was preferable to having sex with a domestic servant or another 'respectable' woman. That is, despite the rhetoric from the pulpits, many of the pre-Reformation assumptions about the utility of prostitutes seems to have remained. What is different is that the city no longer provided its 'whores' with a safe and secure brothel; rather, it drowned them as examples to others.

Some elements of the next case are even more pathetic. In 1567, the city had prosecuted Michée Bourgy from a small village near Nyon. She had been in trouble with Nyon's consistory for 'anticipating' her marriage. She had small children and had been driven to prostitution and theft to support them. Her mother had been burned in 1562 as a witch when she was relatively young. She admitted that she had been a prostitute for four years but denied she had ever worked in Geneva while confessing to a number of minor thefts in the city. Despite torture she denied she was a witch like her mother. She had yelled at Jean Clerc's horse for eating her cabbages but had not touched it or caused it to die. Convicted of the thefts she had confessed to, she was hanged. It is not known what became of her small children.

Even earlier (1543) than these two trials, at the very beginning of the Calvinist reforms in the city, Andrea Ribaud was arrested and 'perpetually banished' for 'having made a trade of fornication'. When asked she said she was not sure why she had been arrested but 'had no doubt it was for fornication'. She freely admitted that she had become a prostitute four years before. She had worked in the 'Stews' but had also plied her trade in shops, stables and other places. Her list of clients is impressive: two servants and a clerk of Amied de la Rive; a valet at the 'Tour Perse' Inn; two men whose names she did not know; a muleteer; servants of Jean des Bors, Pierre des Vignes, Jean de la Chinaz (as well as Jean himself), François Lullin and Baltasar Sept; also, all the servants *chez* André Philippe; the *fils* Pillifray, Ayme Daulnaux, Claude Buttaz, François Deloratel, Claude Conflans and Claude Rolet. As with Louise Maistre, her activities touched a number of prominent families (de la Rive, des Vignes, Lullin) but she seems to have drawn her clients mostly from their domestic staffs rather than the citizenry.

Jacqueme Barbier seems to have served a similar function in the small village of Céligny. She was arrested in 1562. In the course of her trial she was tortured and eventually punished by being privately flogged in the prison. She had had sex for a number of years (as confirmed by an examination conducted by midwives) and had at least one bastard child. Her list of clients, which is almost certainly not complete, included at least four men (which is rather impressive considering that, even today, Céligny is a relatively small village).

In 1570, Jaquemine Chamot fared a bit better. Despite being tortured, she managed to maintain her denials of all the charges against her. She was accused of various fornications and adulteries. Eventually, she was strongly admonished and released. The most significant testimony against her came from Antoina Boreguin, a servant of Pierre Paccot. She said that she had heard that Jaquemine had let Jacques Chavanne sleep in the same bed as her and her husband. She had also been told by another servant that Jaquemine had 'decorated his privates like a bonnet' on one occasion. Finally, she had found Jaquemine's husband, Marquet Petex, weeping in a room. He said he had found his wife with Jean, one of their servants, 'on a bed enjoying one another'. Almost as shockingly, everyone had seen Jean Vandel sleep through last Sunday's sermon with his head on her shoulder.

Another witness also heard that her husband had admonished her asking why she behaved the way she did. She had replied that 'he never did anything and wasn't really her husband nor she his wife', implying that he was either impotent or uninterested in sex; she had also said to him, 'when you have your errands I don't ask you to render an account'. She was known to dance at weddings and to sing dissolute songs. She was also caught in a locked room (after the door was broken in) with a nude, sixteen-year-old boy who said she was 'decorating his privates like a large hat'. The other men told the youth that 'he should refresh himself in the Rhône if he was so hot'.

A number of features of this case are quite interesting. It is clear that this was a very frustrated woman. Her husband was almost certainly impotent. The midwives who examined her said 'for a wife married for a long time she is barely open and had little evidence of having had a man and when it came to the skin associated with deflowering they had found little corruption such that they thought she might not have ever had sex with a man'. What started as a case of possible prostitution seems to have collapsed into a case of attempted – but failed – adulteries. There was not only no evidence of money changing hands, there was also no evidence of sex taking place. Hence, she was admonished and released.

These cases have focused almost wholly on the prostitutes. One should not assume, though, that courts took no interest in the activities of men who solicited women for sex. While it might be acceptable for a man to make use of a 'known' prostitute, it was another matter altogether to try and entice a woman into (a life of) prostitution. The more severe response of the courts to solicitation of '(semi-) respectable' women was made crystal clear to Claude Fichet, a citizen, in 1560. He had come upon a serving girl (who had previously been flogged through the streets) with a bastard babe in her arms and asked her 'how much would you charge to make a child like the one you're carrying in your arms'. He was hauled before the Consistory and then the courts. He was publicly humiliated and then banished for a 'year and a day'.

Claude Perrisod and Michée Planchey (wife of André Tavernier) were both perpetually banished for their involvement in prostitution. They had been seen going into a room together. 'Concerned' neighbours had gathered and broken down the door. They were found, clothed, but obviously involved – they were 'both very red'. Claude had been previously jailed and flogged through the city for adultery and fornication. The crux of this case was that they had started to fool around but had then argued over the amount to be paid

when he had offered her money. He had offered one *sou* and
she had demanded two. In addition to being banished, she
was to accompany Claude as he was, again, flogged through
the streets.

In a mix of domestic fornication and prostitution, Marquet
de Jussel was sued in 1564 by two servants for offering them
money or goods in kind if they would have sex with him.
Mya Allemand had worked for the family for three years
while Claudine Mareschal had been sacked after a few weeks.
Claudine had also been beaten savagely by the couple (neighbours had had to intervene to save her from serious injury).
The wife appears to have known about her husband's importuning of the domestic servants and may have wanted to
confine his attentions to Mya. Moreover, Marquet said
Claudine was a terrible servant. Clearly, no sex had taken
place and though the servants had benefited by some wine
there was no evidence of 'successful' prostitution. Moreover,
Marquet said he only gave wine 'when she had her [period]'
and for no other reason. In the end, the court sent him to jail
for six days and ordered him to appear before the Consistory.

Two brief cases highlight the problems women faced in
making charges of solicitation against men. Two women,
Janette (wife of Jehanton Gerdil) and a certain Berthe
denounced Louis du Molard, a naturalised citizen, for trying
to solicit them with money and presents. He claimed the
money was for 'other services rendered'. The courts decided
the sum was too large for such an explanation and jailed him
for six days. Nicolarde Bossey was not as successful. She
accused Abraham Court and Antoine Chaix, both naturalised
citizens, of soliciting and sexually harassing her. They had
kissed her, touched her breasts and generally talked about sex

in an effort to persuade her. She says this was while her master and mistress were at the 8 o'clock sermon. She also admitted that she had previously fornicated – perhaps in an effort to make her charge more plausible. Unfortunately, the midwives who examined her said she was a virgin. This revelation undermined her testimony as did the strenuous denials of the two men. She was convicted of false witness and jailed for three days.

Finally, in 1570, an interesting case involved a member of one of France's most prominent Protestant families. Lucas Cop, a scion of the family that had produced the rector of the University of Paris credited with starting overt Protestantism in France and a personal physician to Louis XII and Francis I, was arrested for soliciting a domestic servant with offers of money and wine as well as possessing dissolute books. The case actually centred on the books, the most prominent of which were the works of Rabelais (*Gargantua* and *Pantagruel* leading the list), *Les Amours de Roussard* and *Le Courtisan*, many of which he had obtained by trading copies of Calvin's *Commentary on the New Testament* and Latin *Institutes* that he had stolen from the library of Madame de Normandie. As a student, probably a teenager, the court was inclined to be relatively lenient. He was caned in the large hall of the *collège* (upper school) in front of the other students.

A few other brief cases give some evidence of the troubles that authorities faced in trying to control prostitution or the sort of behaviour likely to lead to prostitution. In 1557, Clauda Cavel (aged twenty-four) was jailed for six days. This was the fourth occasion on which she had run away from her guardian's house. She did not wish to live under her brother's control but the court was convinced that she would become a 'libertine'. Likewise, Georgia Besson was thrown out of town for her dissolute behaviour. The judges were convinced that she was a 'lewd' woman but could find no evidence that she was a prostitute or guilty of fornication. However, she was punished for having been found asleep (perhaps drunk) in a trough by the night watch.

A greater problem for authorities was posed by the bathhouses and their lax morals. In 1558, Geneva's judges prosecuted Pierre Jaquet, François Biolley and Alés Biolley (who kept the city's Stews) for allowing men and women to bathe together in the same tubs. They admitted that this was against the city's edicts but had assumed that the rules did not apply to married couples. However, they acknowledged that things could become complicated when a couple was bathing and someone else came in. Even then, they thought this awkward but not untoward as the 'couple' were a unit and therefore nothing bad was likely to happen. The court took the view that this tended to encourage lax morals and should be stopped.

Even more difficult for magistrates was dealing with individuals who simply did not agree with the morals being advanced by a society's rulers. In 1537, immediately after the Reformation, Jacques Villaret was arrested for adultery and fornication. He seems to have taken some of the reformers' sermons about freedom a bit far. He said, freely, that he lived openly with a number of women to whom he was 'married'. He had no idea that fornication was against the law. The magistrates reminded him that as a supporter of the defeated Catholic and Bishop's party he had only been allowed to return on condition that 'he live honestly according to God's commandments, [the city's] ordinances and the new reformation of the faith'. Instead he had lied, perjured himself, seduced a number of women into adultery and fornication, as well as then prostituting some of his 'wives'. He was summarily banished (to find a place where he could live as he wanted).

These cases highlight the difficulties of stopping the oldest of professions. Even in Geneva of the 1550s and '60s, surely one of the most rigorously moral and supervised of cities, the situation was not under control. Not only was the behaviour difficult to find but there were also many cultural reasons for tolerating it. Prostitution dealt with problems arising from large numbers of single men. It allowed married men an outlet for sexual desires without endangering family contracts or inheritance patterns. In the end, there were too many prag-matic arguments for prostitution and too many women driven to it by poverty, if only for a time.

By the end of our period, the pragmatic approach noted before the Reformation had begun to return. After 1730, London police stopped arresting men for soliciting. Also, before 1750 most divorces in England were initiated by women for the sexual vagaries of their husbands. Thereafter, the majority were brought by men against their wives. (This pattern was not, however, replicated elsewhere in Europe.) Also, the very number of prostitutes gives some idea of the inherent problem in trying to eliminate the activity. In 1785–90, nearly 800 prostitutes were arrested in London. The 'seasonal' and opportunistic nature of the trade – which made it even more difficult to regulate – is clear in the pattern of arrests in London. A full 40% of those prosecuted were jailed in May, July and August when the great fairs were held in London.

By 1780, one leading evangelic minister had despaired. Although a champion of houses of reformation and correction for prostitutes he had become convinced that these were not the answer. Nor did he think that greater prosecution and arrest would eliminate the profession. His conclusion was that the problem was not with the supply-side of the trade but with the demand. His solution was to require that men be forced to marry and, thence, financially support any prostitute they were found with. For obvious reasons, his enforced polygamy was unacceptable but it gives some idea of the despair besetting those trying to control and eliminate prostitution.

four

RAPE AND
SEXUAL ASSAULT

In the technical understanding of the law, rape or any violent
sexual assault was a very serious crime indeed. The normal
punishment in the case of conviction was death. However,
the key word is 'conviction'. For example, although rape was
a serious, capital crime in England during the early modern
period, there were actually very few prosecutions and even
fewer convictions. Without the benefit of modern forensic
technology it was very difficult to prove a charge which was,
by its very nature, normally one person's word against another.
In addition, as can be seen in some of the cases that follow,
the victim's character in general, and past sexual activities in
particular, could play a major part in the prosecution. Despite
these many difficulties working against a successful prosecution, convictions were not unknown.

In addition to the obvious difficulties in proving rape or
sexual assault, there were also tensions in early modern culture
working against the severe views articulated by lawyers and

theologians. One can see this alternative idea in Thomas Shadwell's play, *The Virtuoso*, in which the older Sir Formal Trifle pursues a young woman. In an effort to gain her confidence he impersonates a woman. While in drag, he attracts the unwanted advances of Sir Samuel. One of the great moments of broad comedy in the play occurs when Sir Samuel attempts to rape the cross-dressing Sir Formal. Rape, sexual assault and slanderous sexual language, despite legal and moral strictures, were very effective tools of control and humiliation.

It should also be noted from the outset that the term 'rape' was deployed in many places for a category of crimes differing substantially from its use today. For example, the sexual assault of a man by another man was normally seen as a variant of sodomy not rape or sexual assault. In addition, the molesting of a young boy was sodomy not rape, sexual assault or child abuse. However, any sexual assault on a young girl was almost always referred to as a rape not as child abuse. This application of the terms 'rape' and 'sexual assault' hid very different interpretations of what was happening within the actual trials. Thus, the use of 'rape' for an assault on a five-year-old girl did not mean that the crime against her was seen as identical with the rape of an adult woman. Indeed, an examination of the evidence within most trials shows that cases involving children were usually treated the same way regardless of the gender of the victim or the technical term applied by the law to the offence. With this caveat in mind, this chapter will concentrate on cases preserved amongst the abundant criminal dossiers of Geneva which today would be labelled rape and serious sexual assault. Violent sexual acts against children and adolescents will be treated in greater detail in the chapters on child abuse and paederasty, lesbianism, and masturbation in the second section of this volume.

In March and April 1569, Thomas Grillet from France, a religious refugee in Geneva, was prosecuted for trying, first, to seduce his landlady and, when this failed, to assault her. He was flogged and banished for his crimes. He testified that he had come to Geneva 'having been called out of idolatry and papal superstitions and into the knowledge of the Holy Gospel he had applied himself to the study of theology in Geneva and its church to the end that he might, one day, serve as a minister'. Instead of applying himself to his studies he had taken every opportunity he could to seduce and harass his married landlady whose husband came from his home town – he was being funded by a stipend from his home church. He had used moments of prayer for idle chat. He had tried to hug and kiss her at any and every moment. He poured affection on her children and promised her that he would marry her were her husband to die. He had written her poems and tempted her with drink. His every advance had failed. He was, according to the public sentence against him, gripped by 'his impudent love' and was 'guilty and without excuse' for his sexual harassment of Nicole Girard.

The problem the good lady faced was that there were no witnesses to his advances. She testified that she was at her wits' end and begged the judges to do something. He had confessed undying love to her and invited her into his room 'as he had the best affection for her that it was possible to have for a woman'. He even tried to get her to come to his room 'to see some recipes' that he had (an interesting twist on the 'etchings' line). She wisely suggested that he write out the recipe for her and this proved his undoing. On the back of 'the means to make a good aspic' he wrote her a love poem (both survive in the dossier) while taking the precaution to prepare another copy without a poem for her husband's eyes. This allowed her to go to the court with evidence of his affections – if not his actions. (The lawyer, Colladon, who gave an opinion on the case, also noted in passing that the poetry was horrific doggerel.) His duplicity in making two copies of the recipe with and without the poem itself more than proved the case. Grillet, who had been a priest for five years before his conversion and was still a virgin, admitted his harassment and confessed that he merited a serious punishment.

Despite Grillet's many advances, Madame Girard had maintained both her reputation and her virtue. In 1613 Georgea Aricogue (aged twenty), the wife of Pierre Blanc (aged twenty-two), was less fortunate. Her assailant was Guillaume Clemençat (aged twenty-two) a friend of the family. One night he had returned early from guard duty on the city's walls, having paid another soldier to take his place knowing that Pierre was also on duty. He went to the Blanc house and got into bed with Georgea who claimed that she thought it was her husband at first but had then become alarmed and he had fled. The problem for Georgea and the judges was that Susanne le Maistre (aged twenty), Georgea's friend, reported that the next day Georgea had told her that the mystery man in her bed had had sex with her three times. She had realised it was not her husband because 'he had a [penis] much larger than her husband and had a larger member than anyone she knew of'. This raised the question in the minds of the judges that what started as an unwanted seduction or assault quickly became a case of adultery. Georgea strenuously denied having ever said such a thing adding she had 'never even thought' such a thing.

According to Georgea, the man had come to her bed and they had had sex 'not saying a word to one another'. He had then left the bed, she thought, 'to make water'. When he did not return she went looking for him and found there was no one there. The next morning she had asked her husband if he had had a break from guard duty. When he said he had been on duty all night she became alarmed. Initially, they thought that her brother-in-law had accidentally got into the wrong bed but careful questioning during a family meeting had disproved this. When the same man tried the ruse again the next night she had recognised him by his clothes and had cried out. He had fled though not before he was recognised.

Although it is not entirely clear what had happened – and aspects of Susanne's testimony ring true – some fascinating insights into 'normal' marital sex are apparent. It was perfectly normal for the couple to have sex without any dialogue at all and with enough clothing on for Georgea to recognise the clothing of her assailant. Also, the possibility that the brother-in-law might get into the wrong bed in a very crowded dwelling and have sex with the wrong woman seems to have distressed but not surprised anyone. In the end, the court accepted Georgea's version of the events to the extent that Clemençat was banished. However, he had maintained his innocence of the entire affair despite the liberal application of judicial torture.

In 1625, Henri Vautier (aged twenty five) had also managed to assert his innocence despite being tortured. He had been arrested on a charge of trying to rape a cowherd, Pernette

Vernan, whom he had met while passing through Geneva's rural countryside. He admitted that he had met the girl and spoken to her but denied that anything untoward had taken place. There were no eyewitnesses to the assault. However, Martha Dupré (aged fifty), her daughter (Chrestienne Constantin) and two guards (Jean de la Rue and Jean Constantin) all reported on the distressed and disheveled state in which they had found the girl in the aftermath of the alleged attack. Under close questioning and torture, Vautier eventually admitted that he had forcibly touched her breasts but continued to deny that anything else had happened. The prosecution decided that he was guilty of a sexual assault but not rape and banished him forever from the city on pain of death.

At the end of the sixteenth century another interesting case occurred. Jacquemin Curtet (also known as Bocard, aged twenty-two), a soldier in the company of Capt. Pellissari, was accused of raping Pernette de Souget, a twenty-five-year-old chambermaid. She testified that she had cried out so loud that her mistress had come running and found her in floods of tears saying she had just been raped by a soldier who was 'tall and dark-complexioned wearing leather and a long hat', young and clean shaven. He was a cavalryman not a foot soldier.

The mistress, Mya Folliex (aged forty-five), made no mention of a scream and was much more concerned to detail the damage done by the soldiers quartered on the farmstead. She had gone there from Geneva with Pernette to try to limit the damage. The dozen or so soldiers were mostly cavalrymen and had caused considerable damage and been very insolent in their treatment of herself and her chambermaid.

In part, she confirmed Pernette's general impressions of the situation but in crucial details her testimony failed to support Pernette's account.

Four of the soldiers then gave testimony. They all agreed that Pernette had been in Curtet's room, where he had made up a straw pallet. However, they testified that he had only been in the room with her for about fifteen minutes and that the door had always been open. More importantly, although Pernette had left the room in obvious distress (crying) there had been no screams and no accusations were made at the time. Pernette was then re-questioned and admitted that she had fornicated in the past – with a Savoyard soldier, an enemy of the city. At the court's request she was then examined by two midwives (or *sages femmes*) who reported that she was pregnant and had had sex often; 'she was well and truly open'. They could not confirm any sign of force.

This case completely baffled the judges. Pernette was adamant that she had been raped while all the other evidence implied that the circumstances were such that this was very unlikely (the open door was key). The court decided to widen the investigation to include others from around the farmstead. François de la Rive (aged thirty) and his wife, Michée, as well as Louis Bertet (a forty-year-old labourer) and Abraham Bechod were all questioned. François and Abraham were citizens and the latter was also a civic official. Their testimony simply complicated the case further while offering the glimmer of an explanation. They had all met Pernette on the road immediately after the alleged attack and were convinced that there had been no rape. However, they did say that about a year before, when the region had been occupied by enemy soldiers, Pernette had been raped on a number of occasions by Savoyard troops from Piedmont and Spain. One time, a Savoyard cavalry captain had intervened and driven off the assailant.

The court eventually came to the conclusion that Curtet was innocent and he was released. However, under the strict reading of the law, Pernette should have been liable for the punishment for rape (death) as Geneva's law decreed that any false witness would incur the penalty of the person falsely accused. Despite Pernette's obvious perjury no action was taken against her. Instead the judges seem to have decided that her previous rape had induced a trauma which had led her to fear all soldiers and this had produced the false, 'hysterical' accusation when she accidentally found herself alone in a room with a cavalryman. They placed her in the care of her neighbours and gave explicit instructions that she be kept from the company of soldiers.

Bearing in mind the lack of forensic technology and the lack of witnesses, the judges show a consistent willingness to take seriously the accusations of these female victims. Nevertheless, as the case of the 'Aspic Recipe' shows, there was a universal understanding that a charge of sexual harassment or assault was much easier to make if there was some corroborating evidence. The case of the cavalryman also shows some implicit awareness of the impact of a traumatic rape on the mind of the victim. Indeed, the willingness of the judges to banish the alleged assailants suggests that they preferred to err on the side of caution when reacting to an accusation of sexual assault by a woman.

Sexual assault and rape were not the only ways in which the reputation and virtue of a woman could be impugned. Indeed, words and accusations *about* a woman could have as

disastrous an effect as actual sexual misdeeds whether voluntary or not. And, it is worth noting that the case of the 'Well-
Endowed Mystery Man' was as much about an attempt by
the 'wronged' husband to recover his wife's honour as it was
to punish the assailant. At all cost, there could be no thought
that a woman had been even partially complicit in an attack.
This explains the reaction of women and their families to
slanderous assaults of a sexual nature on their honour and
character.

In 1624, Jacques Jasard and his wife, Jeanne Chanay, brought
a case against Blaise Gueirod 'for impugning the honour of
Jeanne and beating her'. Jacques alleged that about 7 o'clock
the previous evening, Blaise had struck Jeanne twice in the
head, knocking her to the ground. On any number of previous occasions he had tried to put his hand up her skirt including once in her own mother's house. Her cries had brought
her mother to her rescue. Rebuffed, he struck her and gave
her a bloody nose. In addition to these and other physical and
sexual assaults on her person, Blaise always called her – loudly
– a 'whore' in public.

Numerous neighbours attested to Blaise's shocking and
violent behaviour against Jeanne. One, Charlotte Van (the
thirty-two-year-old wife of Antoine Platan, citizen and master
goldsmith) related that she had rebuked Blaise for referring
to Jeanne as a 'whore' and he had said, he 'could prove it
[because] Jeanne's house is a whorehouse and brothel'. For
his part, Blaise (aged twenty-five) said that he was angry with
Jacques for refusing to return some items he had borrowed.
He admitted he had threatened to strike Jeanne but denied
that he had perpetrated any assault, whether physical or
sexual. The court decided that the preponderance of evidence

was against Blaise. He was made to beg for mercy in public and banished on pain of being flogged. However, in addition to these normal punishments, he was also ordered to apologise publicly to Jeanne and Jacques.

A few years later, in 1631, three men (brothers David and Abraham Guainier, aged twenty-nine and thirty respectively, and Pierre Caillati, aged twenty-one) were messing around in the countryside with an arquebuse and generally being rowdy. Pernette de Michaille (aged twenty-two, wife of Michel du Prala, aged forty) remonstrated with them for their behaviour. They gave as good as they got and Pernette's husband then got involved. According to the three men he had struck Pierre with a stone and he had struck back using the gun as a club when he saw his own blood. Michel and Pernette said that the men had called her a 'whore' and had attacked the couple with the hilts of their swords. Michel, in coming to the rescue of his wife, was putting into practice the sort of advice epitomised in Gouge's *Domestical Duties* (1622): '[when] mischiefe… is intended or practiced against [his wife], [a husband] must be a tower of defense to protect her'.

At this point the Santoux family came along. The mother (Françoise Pichard, aged thirty-five) was on horseback while her husband (Pierre Santoux, aged forty-five) and son (Isaac, aged eighteen) were on foot. They intervened in the brawl. The defendants said that Françoise had come off her horse at them 'like a mad woman' and they had struck her and her husband in self-defence. The court was amazed to find three grown men responsible for striking not only two other men but two women. They were all fined (and made to apologise); Pierre did not have enough money to pay so he was confined in the dungeons for three days.

These two cases give some idea of the place of words in early modern culture. They also show the level of casual violence and sexual harassment. Impugning the honour of a woman was an easy way to attack both her and her family. Also, these cases demonstrate the enthusiasm for people to admonish one another in the street and to intervene in problematic situations. In a world without police it was essential that everyone 'do their part'. However, the other side of this willingness to become involved was that it was often deeply resented by one or both sides of a dispute and, as a result, a simple exchange of words between two people could easily escalate into a wider debate if not a full-blown riot. In that context the physical assaulting and sexual harassing of a woman, as well as the use of sexually loaded words, played an important part.

Likewise, any assault on a pregnant woman, though clearly not sexual assault or rape, was seen as being especially reprehensible. In these cases, women were viewed differently, not because they were the 'weaker sex' but because of their specific role as mother. Her sex, in the sense of her procreative and maternal role rather than her gender, came to the fore. A number of cases from Westminster in London serve to highlight the stress that courts placed on the procreative, maternal and sexual role of women, especially wives.

On 11 August 1690 John Brock was bound over for trial for pouring water on Elinor, wife of John Hudson, who 'being bigg with child… whereby she is in danger to miscarry'. It was a widely held belief that any severe shock could cause a woman to miscarry or produce a deformed child. Likewise, most people believed that a miscarriage would complicate if not preclude any future pregnancies. Timothy Corker was also held for assaulting Elizabeth Smith, 'she being great with child whereby she is dangerously ill'. In 1701, Margaret Steward brought a more serious charge against William Smith for 'assaulting and frightning of her and threatning to throw her downe staires whereby she hath miscarryed of a child wherewith she was about two monthe gone'. A similar accusation was laid by Mrs Williams against her husband who 'many times assaulted, brate and bruised her, whereby she has several times miscaryed'.

A few words of caution are necessary in any interpretation of this type of assault against the 'sexuality' of a woman. First, of the cases that note a pregnancy, 31% of the assailants were other women. Also, a miscarriage was not always seen as crucial to a case. As Richard Burn advised in his guidebook to magistrates, *Justice of the Peace and Parish Officer* (1755): '[On bastardy], if a woman be quick [the child had moved] or great [near delivery] with child... [and] if man strike her, whereby the child within her is killed, tho' it be a great crime, yet it is not murder or manslaughter by the law of England'. On the other hand, in most Continental countries causing the miscarriage of a 'quick child' carried the death penalty while the death of an 'unquickened' foetus merited only a fine. The stress on a moving foetus simply highlights the lack of gynecological sophistication (it was not always clear a woman was pregnant early on) as well as the temptation to pretend a pregnancy.

The claim to being pregnant was very important. In assault cases it might well encourage the judge or jury to award higher damages. When the woman was a defendant it almost always delayed or obviated judicial torture, corporal punishment or the death penalty. There was widespread awareness of the means by which a woman might use her procreative and sexual role to defend or better her position before the law. An excellent example of this comes from Henry Fielding's *Joseph Andrews* (1742). The young and pretty Fanny Goodwill when wrongly accused of theft received an interesting offer from a friend of the judge: 'if she had not provided herself a great Belly, he was at her service'. Moreover, there was a widespread view that conception could only take place if ejaculation (i.e., an orgasm) took place in both the man and woman. As such, a woman claiming rape resulting in pregnancy had her case seriously undermined since her condition showed that she had 'enjoyed' the sexual act. The repugnant offer to Fanny as well as the shocking views on conception neatly link pregnancy and female sexuality with sexual harassment and assault.

It is important to remember, though, that rape and sexual assault could result in severe punishments despite the lack of forensic evidence or cultural views tolerating fairly general sexual harassment of women. Thus far we have concentrated on sexual assault and harassment as well as the use of sexually insulting language. In the next two cases, the emphasis will be on rape itself. In the first (1568), Jean-Baptiste Payerni, a former priest, was beheaded for adultery and rape. In the second (1562), Martin Leschière was drowned for attempted rape and adultery.

In Payerni's case, two of his serving girls testified against him. Clauda Bourbon had been subjected to repeated assaults both verbal and physical in her master's house and even in the homes of others when she was accompanying the family on social and business visits. Marie Saxod told a similar story.

Payerni's wife also testified that she had found him in a compromising position with another servant, Jeanne du Chesme, who confessed that his repeated attentions and threats had finally been successful.

Under intense questioning but without the use of torture, Payerni told his story. He had fled Cremona where he had been a priest to come to Geneva and live as a Protestant. However, he had repeatedly assaulted and harassed his three young maids. While in the country, on the pretext of picking fruit, he had attempted to rape Marie. Eventually, Jeanne had succumbed to his efforts and, afterwards, had admonished him. He had recognised his fault and apologised but later returned to his original behaviour.

Colladon's legal advice was clear in its conclusion but less precise about the reasoning. He strongly recommended that Payerni should be executed; he was beheaded and exposed on the gibbet. However, Colladon was not sure that rape was the actual crime. Payerni was certainly guilty of adultery but Jeanne had submitted. In the end, the court decided that this was 'adultery and fornication by force' but stopped short of calling it rape. Finally, Colladon also thought that Payerni deserved a severe penalty because 'he had given his wife [and perhaps Jeanne] an incurable [venereal] disease which is a great wrong and damage'.

The sentence against Martin Leschière, in 1562, lists his extensive crimes:

> You have for a long time been of bad conversation and a dissolute and wasteful life to the great scandal of this reformed church and being false and disloyal to the [marriage] promises made to your wife you have

abandoned yourself to commit the detestable crime of fornication and adultery and many other acts infamous to, and unworthy of, a Christian man. Likewise, you have long persisted in this despite being repeatedly and sufficiently admonished by the worthy members of the Consistory and by this court... and, what is worse, you have also committed the horrible and detestable crime of rape in trying to force violence on a girl, very young and inno- cent, trying to penetrate her to have your carnal way perse- vering in your disorderly and evil affection and concupiscence against the order of nature which ought to be inviolable to everyone.

His career was indeed impressive. He had been admonished three times in 1553 by the Consistory for two acts of forni- cation. In 1557, he was rebuked for insolence to the elders and ministers of the Consistory. Twice in 1559 he was exam- ined for fornication and blasphemy; he was handed over to the secular arm and banished. In 1560 he was prosecuted twice for breaking his banishment (he said he preferred to die in Geneva than in a 'Papist country'). It is an amazing comment both on the state's patience and, perhaps, Martin's character that his behaviour was tolerated so long. In the end, his attempt to rape Madeleine (aged twelve) was a crime too far. It was clear that no penetration had taken place. He had thrown her on to a bed of straw, raised her skirts and pressed himself against her but said that he had repented of his act at that moment and stopped; Madeleine confirmed that he had halted the assault. This momentary attack of conscience may give some insight into the character that the judges, elders and ministers had seen — and tolerated — for so long.

Nevertheless, patience was at an end and Martin was drowned for his present crimes as well as his dissolute life and past offences.

Finally, one must not forget that men could also be victims of rape, sexual assault and harassment. Four brief cases from Geneva will suffice to give some idea of how societies, in general, and their judges dealt with sexual attacks by men on men. The first case from 1615 is complicated by multiple charges against the defendant, Jean Bourier (aged sixty-two). He was accused of attempted sodomy, sodomy, and witch-craft. Initially, he was arrested for causing, through sorcery, the illness of Sara (aged forty), wife of Jean Guillan (aged thirty). As was their wont in witchcraft trials, the judges sought depo-sitions from everyone who knew the defendant to see if the charge might be true. Rather than uncovering a known sorcerer, the court found that Jean was widely known for sexually harassing men.

Samuel Coindi (aged forty) testified that three years before, while leaving church, Jean had come up behind him and fondled him. Jean Veillard (aged fifty-three) said that he had been told that 'Bourier never touches woman' and had been seen molesting a cow in a stable. Samuel Bailliard (aged thirty) reported that three years ago, Jean had groped one of his customers in his shop. Jean de la Plans (aged forty) had heard these comments as rumours but also said that his maid (Mathhia) had seen Jean, through an open window, playing with himself under a table; the maid confirmed the report. A soldier, Jacques Delmanille (aged thirty-five) said two other soldiers had warned him of Jean who had harassed them so much they had had to threaten to strike him. Mathelin Perren (aged thirty-nine) told how three years before Jean had lifted his coat and fondled him. Nicolas Pain (aged forty) testified that Jean had put his hand in Nicolas' pocket and, when he was stopped, said he was only looking for a handkerchief.

This case is fascinating for showing (as did many of those relating to assault and harassment of women) the lack of enthusiasm in individuals for involving the state in these types of situations. By and large, for three years, Jean had been fairly widely known for sexually harassing and assaulting other men. None of these men complained to the law. Instead, they simply repulsed his advances. In fact, the court discovered that he had been prosecuted thirty years before (when he was about thirty) for sodomy and ten years before for harassing David Rammier in front of a church. Before the case could proceed, Jean died in jail. The public sentence against him said that:

> having forgotten all faith in God and natural instinct, he
> had abandoned himself to the execrable crime of sodomy...
> [and that] his dead body should be dragged on a sledge in
> fulfillment of supreme justice to the place of Plainpalais
> [the city's slaughteryard] and there to be burnt and reduced
> to ashes in the normal fashion to serve as an example to
> those who would want to commit similar crimes. Further,
> a fine of 200 écus should be taken from his estate.

Although he seems not actually to have committed sodomy, there is no doubt that his harassment and assaults would have led to his execution.

Two years before, in 1613, Mermet Pastour had been condemned to public humiliation and banished on pain of death for his 'impudent acts and suspicion of sodomy'. Mermet was known for his problems with his wife including his physical assaults on her. On one occasion he had yelled out a window to another man, 'does your wife have as big an arsehole [as my wife]?' He seemed to think that his wife was having an affair since he called her 'Lady Cat-Whore' and had shouted at the door of her supposed lover, 'come out, come out, you sinful man from your house' and threatened to kill him. This dispute was the occasion for the spotlight of official investigation to fall on Mermet's life – with disastrous consequences for him.

A large number of witnesses confirmed Mermet's violent and vicious temper and the broad outline of his attacks on his wife and the alleged lover, Rollet Choppin. However, Rollet also related that Mermet had made sexual advances on a servant (de la Planche) of David Colladon, a syndic. He had also harassed George Gaudi and another servant named Guillaume. He had exposed himself, fondled himself and then thrown the startled Guillaume to the ground in an effort to rape him. Guillaume had resisted violently and said 'if [you] don't stop, I'll kill you'. Guillaume Mermet (aged thirty-four), Nicolas de la Planche (aged twenty-four) and George Gaudi (aged twenty-seven) confirmed Rollet's testimony. Also, Nicolas Gallex (aged twenty-five) reported that he had been a dinner guest at Mermet's. He testified that 'after dinner he had been standing near the fire to warm himself and Pastour was standing near him and the said Pastour took his member out of his flies and fondling himself with one hand, with the other hand he had taken hold of the member of the witness'. Again, the men chose to deal with these advances themselves. This case, as the first one, came to the attention of the state not because of sexual harassment and assault but because of other, unrelated charges.

In our third case, we see a direct appeal to the state by a victim. In 1569, Archambaud Girard (aged nineteen) brought a charge against Jerome Spada (aged twenty-five, from Brescia). They were sharing a bed and three different times, about midnight, the Italian had pressed himself against Archambaud and molested him. However, the testimony from others in the inn seemed to suggest that Archambaud was lying. In addition, he was suspected of falsely accusing 'men of quality' of theft. The others in the room said the two men had shared a bed two nights and there had been no apparent problems. Also, the hostess of the inn said she had searched the sheets and there was no sign of semen or any other stain which might have resulted from sexual activity. For his part, Jerome said that he had slept closely to the youth because he thought he was feverish and needed comfort. In his defence, he also said he was unable to assault anyone as he was suffering the ravages of 'the Naples malady' (venereal disease). The city's chief legal advisor, Colladon, suggested that Archambaud, for being a false witness in a capital crime could be put to death but thought his age (and perhaps his health) mitigated against the harsher penalty. Also, Jerome was hardly a paragon of virtue as his health testified. He recommended that both should be banished; the court concurred.

The final case is probably the best in presenting a stereotypical example of an actual sexual assault by a man against a man. It also provides one of the most explicit and defiant statements by an accused sodomite. In 1617, Jean de la Rue, aged an impressive eighty, was arrested for making a pass at a youth, Balthasar, with whom he had shared a bed for several nights in an inn. Balthasar had promptly reported the assault. Jean readily confessed the crime. When he was asked how long he had been doing this sort of thing, he said, 'for years'. Considering the reticence of male victims of sexual harassment and assault that we have seen above, this is completely believable. When asked why he kept trying to have sex with men, he said, 'for pleasure, for food, and because of his poverty'. For having 'confessed that for many years he had abandoned himself to committing the horrible crime of sodomy, against nature, with many people outwith this city' he was executed.

Collectively, these cases make it clear that rape, sexual assault, harassment and slander of a person's sexual reputation were areas that greatly concerned early modern society but were very difficult for courts to treat. In making judgments, the courts relied on witnesses, the past character of defendants and plaintiffs, and the general credibility of the charge. In many cases they seemed to prefer to err on the side of caution and punish the defendant, though most often short of death. Also, sexual assault and harassment against women was treated much more leniently than against men. Perhaps this simply exposes an underlying assumption that a woman's resistance in an assault was always questionable while it was implicitly accepted that no man would willingly tolerate sexual advances, let alone an assault, from another man.

II

Unnatural Sex

five

SODOMITES AND
MALE SEXUAL DEVIANCE

In a numerical sense, the crimes discussed in Part One of this volume far exceeded those to follow. Indeed, fornication and adultery trials as a whole probably were greater than all the rest put together. However, the relative infrequency of trials for 'unnatural' sex did not lessen their importance. The fact is that these were the showcase sex crimes through the period under examination. If the general public were amused, titillated or shocked by the sins we have already considered they were absolutely mesmerised and horrified by the public denunciations of perpetrators of the various forms of sodomy.

Theoretically, sodomy was a fairly general term for most types of crime that were deemed to be 'against nature'. In effect, this meant sexual relations that were non-procreative. By the middle ages, most jurists and theologians had subdivided sodomy into four general categories: sex between men, sex with animals, non-procreative sex between men and women, and masturbation. However, in practice even procreative sex could be considered unnatural if it was in any position other than the missionary (face-to-face, man on top, woman on her back).

There was also a more narrow use of the term sodomy. This was its application almost wholly to sex between males. Even here there were possibilities for confusion and national variations. In some countries, all genital contact between males might be considered sodomitical. In other places, it was necessary to prove anal penetration and ejaculation for a successful prosecution. Again though, practice differed from legal definitions. The reality was that sodomy (or buggery) was most often used to refer to any genital contact between individuals of the same sex (though lesbianism was extremely rare and only seems to have been included as an afterthought). Most of the other crimes technically under the rubric of sodomy had more specific terms (e.g., bestiality, masturbation) which were used more frequently. This chapter will focus on the use of sodomy and buggery to refer to genital contact between men.

Before considering individual cases, some general comments about male sexual deviance are crucial. Most importantly, social and cultural attitudes to sex between men were not monolithic across Europe, nor did they remain consistent over time. The historian Randolph Trumbach has made some trenchant observations which serve as signposts for the discussion to follow. He begins by noting that sodomy originally had the wide range of meanings just noted. However,

> In the eighteenth century [sodomy] came to refer increasingly to male homosexual relations alone. This sort of

sodomite was presumed to have no interest in women. By contrast, his seventeenth-century counterpart would have been found with his whore on one arm and his catamite on the other. The new exclusive adult sodomite was also supposed to be effeminate, and effeminacy lost its seventeenth-century meaning of referring both to cross-dressing boys and to men enervated by too great a sexual interest in women. The majority of eighteenth-century men therefore constructed their masculinity around their avoidance of the sodomite's role and, instead, fervently pursued women and, of course, prostitutes.

Lords Stanhope and Shaftesbury, in the 1720s, seemingly suffered no ill effects from being reputed for an interest in women and adolescent males. Later in the century, Lords Hervey and Germain found their tastes rejected by society. Previously, to be sexually daring meant having sex with just about anyone (especially, women and adolescent males). By the middle of the eighteenth century, 'men' only desired women. The sodomite became a 'creature' who only desired men and became known as a 'molly', a word that had originally meant 'whore'. The Restoration rake, so much a feature of society and the stage of the late seventeenth century was 'bisexual' in practice. This type of libertinism had begun to disappear from the stage by the 1690s and society more generally soon thereafter. One of the last gasps of this libertine attitude to sexual pleasure came from the mouth of a convicted 'sodomite' in London (1726) who said: 'I think it no crime in making what use I please with my own body'.

It is, of course, important to remember that even in this earlier period, the attitudes were not necessarily tolerant to this sort of libertinism. For example, dramatic representations of sexual libertinism could serve as much to reinforce social prejudices as to present a type of tolerance. Nevertheless, the representations are interesting in the type of behaviour that is seen as acceptable for the stage. Linceus in Marston's *Cynicke Satyre* (1599) was noted for 'fayre appendant whore' and 'sodome beastliness'. In Nathaniel Lee's *Princess of Cleves* (1689) the hero pursues women and his page (who also indulges in relations with both sexes). One of the last examples of this sort of libertine is seen in G.G. Landsdowne's *The She-Gallants* (1696) where a foppish character, considering the beauties of a handsome youth masquerading as a women calls him/her 'a Rump-Jewel for a Prince' but later laments the plague of 'pale-fac'd catamites' besetting the city. This libertinism was more than simply a dramatic device; Thomas Shadwell, in 1682, mocked Dryden (seemingly without offence) for wanting to bugger any gender. But, this interest in women and adolescent males was the product of an entirely different mindset and worldview from that of the eighteenth-century Dutch preacher who defended his interest in men alone as 'proper to his nature'.

The alterations to categories and constructions of gender is, perhaps, getting a bit ahead of the story. The Renaissance and, in particular, Italy is the place to begin any discussion of male, same-sex desire. Italy was, after all, seen throughout the period from the Renaissance to the Enlightenment as the fount of sodomy. As the preface to *The Tryal and Condemnation... of Castelhaven... [in] 1631* (1649) put it, sodomy was spreading having been 'Translated from the *Sadomitical* Original, or from the *Turkish* and *Italian* copies into *English*'. Indeed, Venice convicted 110 sodomites in the period 1448–69. There seems little doubt that social attitudes to sodomy were more tolerant in Renaissance Italy than elsewhere in Europe until the eighteenth century. Almost certainly this is related to a complex mixture of the size of urban environments, levels of education, cultural attachments to classical learning and sophistication, and wealth. Even higher numbers were uncovered in Florence during the fifteenth and early sixteenth centuries when the city instituted a special police force charged solely with the eradication of sodomy.

Still, these numbers should not be exaggerated. In both cases, the authorities intentionally turned their attention to the crime. Between 1565 and 1640, eighty cases appealed to the Paris *parlement* resulted in the execution of sodomites. In Geneva (1555–1678), a town of no more than 20,000 souls, thirty sodomites were executed. The Dutch in the period 1750–1800 prosecuted 269 sodomites. All things being the same, these numbers do not necessarily imply that the activity became more or less common as time passed. They do seem to suggest that there was a level of sodomitical activity there to be discovered should a state's magistrates desire to find it.

For obvious reasons relating to the survival of documents, there is better evidence of sodomitical activity in the eighteenth century than earlier. However, the criminal court records of Geneva are, as we have seen, especially good. Therefore, before turning to other nations (especially England), it would seem useful to examine some sodomy cases from sixteenth- and early seventeenth-century Geneva. Although these cases give little evidence of the alteration to cultural constructions of sodomy over time, they do demonstrate the fascination judges had with unnatural sex and the level of detail that can survive from this earlier period.

In 1551, Jean Fontanna and François Puthod were arrested for 'inappropriate acts' initiated by Fontanna. The best evidence suggests that Fontanna was in his mid-forties while Puthod gave his age as about nineteen. He lived in the Fontanna house though he does not appear to have been a servant. Presumably, he was either a lodger or a ward of some sort. The two had come to the attention of the court when they were seen 'wrestling' nude in a garden by Jacques Bonna, Jean-Philibert Bonna and Gaspard Magistri. Their behaviour was so peculiar that, at a distance, the witnesses had originally assumed they were watching a man and woman have sex. Under intense questioning, the court discovered that the two had been engaged in sexual relations for about a year even though Fontanna had a wife and child. Fontanna admitted that they had mutually masturbated and engaged in inter-crural sex (between Puthod's thighs) and frottage. However, they both specifically denied that anal penetration had taken place, ever. The relationship had begun after Fontanna had noticed, while Puthod was bathing that 'he had an enormous member'. Indeed, he told Puthod, on a number of occasions that 'you have a large cock'. Puthod told the court that he did not know if what they had done was 'good or bad, but if bad he begged for mercy and forgiveness'. Legal advice from Colladon and Laurent de Normandie said that, at the very least, Fontanna should be executed and Puthod, after being made to assist in the execution, should be banished forever on pain of death. Chevallier, who was a native Genevan (the other two lawyers were French) took a more lenient line. He simply suggested that Fontanna should be punished more harshly (not only for sodomy but also 'the sin of Onan', masturbation) and Puthod's age and 'ignorance' should be taken into account. The resulting sentence was a mix of the two. Fontanna was ordered to be chained to a large stone for a year and a day and Puthod was banished. There is some evidence, though, to suggest that Fontanna was, in fact, executed.

Indeed, the evidence for Fontanna's execution for relapsing into sodomy comes a decade later in the case of Guillaume Branlard and Balthasar Ramel. Branlard, aged thirty-three, admitted to having seduced and sodomised Ramel who was only about sixteen. While this might seem a case more appropriate to the chapter on paederasty to follow, Branlard also confessed that he had had sex with Fontanna on a number of occasions. Moreover, he was vividly aware of the penalty for the crime as he had seen Fontanna executed about six years previously. He claimed that he had been 'seduced by Satan and begged God for mercy'. The legal advice, which the court accepted, said that Branlard should be drowned in the Rhône and Ramel (for allowing Branlard's attentions) should be banished.

That same year a much more complex and slightly amusing case confronted the city's judges. Thomas de Reancourt and Jacques Beudant were arrested. Numerous witnesses testified that Thomas regularly fondled and groped men, especially during and immediately after church services. He was also known to expose himself at the oddest and most public of times. It seems that a number of individuals decided that something had to be done and convinced Beudant, who was only eighteen, to go along with Thomas' advances long enough to get him into a room. Once there, they would burst in and catch Thomas, *in flagrante*. The court thought this type of do-it-yourself sting operation was objectionable and possibly criminal and delayed proceedings while some of those involved were questioned. They were also amazed that Jacques had agreed and had allowed the situation to evolve to the point that he eventually had Thomas' tongue in his mouth and his hands groping his bottom. The legal opinions had no greater luck in deciding what to do. They noted Beudant's youth and that Reancourt was married with children. There seems to be a general awareness that Reancourt may have had some slight mental impairment. Indeed, Beudant's age and Reancourt's mental stability seem to have saved their lives. In the end, both were banished though Reancourt on pain of death and Beudant on pain of being flogged.

These cases highlight two important features of many sodomy trials. Firstly the seeming ability of the behaviour, especially sexual harassment, to continue for a while before coming to the attention of the courts. Secondly, the difficulty that courts had with deciding on an age of accountability. Each of the cases above involved a teenager who today would be seen as legally responsible. Still, the courts took a more lenient view. The amount of detail of sexual acts as well as the difficulty presented to lawyers by behaviour which would today be seen as a sign of mental instability is also apparent.

Other cases required the courts to make decisions worthy of Solomon. In 1565, Nicolas Garnier and his fellow servant Jean Lichière were arrested. Their master, Nicolas Hiasson, reported that one morning about 5 o'clock he had come to wake the two servants. He had heard 'them corrupting themselves together and that the said [Garnier] say that he had troubled one of the blankets on the bed and the said Jean wanted to take him, the said Jean, among other things called the said Nicolas a bugger to which the said Nicolas said "that's you yourself"'. Confronted, the two began to accuse one another of molestation. During the trial Nicolas said that Jean had tried to have sex with him in their shared bed and he also admitted that Jean had said to him that 'he would be better to marry than to burn'. When he resisted, Jean had punched him and given him a bloody nose. Jean, for his part, turned the story around and said that Nicolas had assaulted him lacerating and bruising his arms. They were both religious refugees and said they were virgins. Eventually they both admitted that they had placed their penises between one another's thighs. The court decided that no penetration or ejaculation had taken place and could not identify who actually initiated the activity. As a result, the judges were content to banish both on suspicion of sodomy. Although brief and complex, this case does give an interesting insight into the private life of two workers in their shared room.

Another vignette, in 1568, shows a similar situation but one in which one roommate was less willing to participate in the sexual antics. Jean de la Tour's roommate, Amied Messier, reported him for sexual advances. According to de la Tour, they had 'while abed, been masturbating and [Jean] asked [Amied] to be allowed to ejaculate in/at his ass and that they were both as erect as with a women but [Amied] refused'. He also admitted that he had done this before with success but he truly thought he had been arrested on suspicion of fornication because he was 'very ill with [a venereal disease]'. He also said that he had lost his virginity when he was about fifteen (his age at the time of the trial is not known) to a teacher in Aoste when he was the page of Mon. the Comte de Chalons. He had not allowed penetration only intercrural sex even though the teacher had had him in bed all night and solicited him constantly. Later, in Lyon, he had been repeatedly penetrated by three Italians in turn as a result of which he had been very unwell. Finally, he confessed that he had once had sex with a woman, but only the once. Although his actual behaviour in Geneva did not differ greatly from that of the two men in the previous case, the court decided that his overall sexual history merited a more severe punishment; he was drowned.

It is clear in these trials that there is no obvious association of sodomy with any particular type of individual behaviour. That is, the courts do not have in mind a stereotype of a 'sodomite'. The men come from a range of professions and most are poorer artisans. Their activity seems either to be opportunistically associated with the sharing of a bed in a city crowded with male religious refugees or the result of long-term practices. However, the courts do not think that sodomitical acts are just one-off events. They want to know if any given defendant has had sex with a woman or produced children. They also assume there may be some contact with Italians or Italy (that is, classicised, Italian Renaissance culture). They also assume that previous sexual acts of sodomy are evidence of a predilection for the behaviour. In other words, they do seem to think that some people have 'appetites' that incline them to one sex or another. Clearly though, they think that 'giving oneself over' to these appetites is largely a matter of the will and habit.

This lack of a stereotype accompanied by certain assumptions about repeated behaviour seems to underlie the reports by Nuno de Guzman in 1530. Writing of a recent battle with an Amerindian tribe in South America, he related that the very last soldier to surrender 'fought most courageously, was a man in the [clothes] of a woman, [who] confessed that from a child he had gotten his living by that filthiness, for which I caused him to be burned'.

During the course of the seventeenth century one sees, at least in English drama, the emergence of the image of the 'fop' already commented on above. Still, the cases from this period seem to suggest that the earlier understanding of sodomitical acts survived. There was no assumption of a particular type of behaviour nor any necessary thought that a sodomite will, by definition, be wholly interested in his own sex.

Certainly, the trial and arrest of Mervin Touchet, Lord Audley, Earl of Castlehaven in 1631 makes this point. He is displayed as a sexual libertine and pervert. Among his many perversions was sodomy. He was accused (and later executed) for having had sex with a number of his adult male servants. His attentions then, in opposition to the fop of the stage, was not for adolescent males but full-grown men. He tried to argue that, under a strict interpretation of the law, the testimony against him only pointed to intercrural sex, not penetration. Thus, he had not committed buggery. The court ruled that the *sine qua non* of buggery was ejaculation not penetration. However, for most of his peers in the House of Lords sitting in judgment against him the shocking aspect of his behaviour was not sex with servants (since that was simply an extreme extension of the hierarchical ordering of society). Rather, they were appalled that he had held down his wife, Catherine, while his favourite servant had obeyed his command to force her. In addition, he had helped the servant rape his twelve-year-old daughter-in-law so that he might have an heir by the servant rather than his son. As the girl was so young the servant related that the earl had had to apply lubricant to them to allow the rape to proceed. The diverse perversions of this case, of which sodomy was but one (and perhaps the least) were such that even Charles I was forced to abandon his good friend and favourite to the executioner.

The prevailing ambivalence to, and general toleration of, some sorts of sodomitical activity (most notably paederasty) as well as a more fluid understanding of the correct objects of masculine desire is evident throughout most of the seventeenth century. For example, Pepys wrote (in the 1660s) of the actor Edward Kynaston, who was known for his portrayal of women, that he was both 'the prettiest woman in the whole house' and 'the handsomest man'. That he was also widely rumoured to be the catamite of the Duke of Buckingham seems not to have had any impact on his popular appeal. By the end of the century this situation was changing. One example of this alteration was the introduction of specific words for the passive (berdache) and active (sodomite) participant in sodomy. Berdache was considerably more pejorative than catamite and, more importantly, did not have the implicit association with paederasty. So great had been the cultural shift that John Dennis in his *Usefulness of the Stage* (1698), written in response to Jeremy Collier's attack on the depraved morality of the theatre, said that 'that unnatural sin, which is another growing vice of the Age... [was] either never mentioned [by the stage] or mentioned with the last Detestation'. The vice, of course, was sodomy and it was one of the 'four reigning vices' in England (along with, perhaps bizarrely considering the discussion, 'the love of women', 'drinking' and 'gambling').

Seventeenth-century Genevan trials display no real change from those of the earlier century. Two will suffice to show the character of the cases from this century. However, two points must be made. First, after mid-century there are no more executions in Geneva for 'crimes against nature' and, indeed, there are no trials at all until the mid- to late eighteenth century. Second, as we shall see, the century started with the accidental discovery of an extensive network of sodomites in the city. Before looking at the peculiar case of Pierre Canal and his friends, let us examine two 'normal' cases of 'abnormal' sexual activity.

In 1621, Louis Dorenges (aged fifty) was arrested for sodomy (and sorcery). Claude Morel (aged twenty-three) reported that he had taken a note to Louis' employer and, while spending the night in the same bed, Louis had tried to molest him. Another witness, Bernard, said that Louis had also sexually assaulted him a few years before when he was aged fifteen. Claude Jaquema testified that, ten years previously, Louis had groped him in bed. Although he initially denied the accusations, Louis then said, that 'to ease his conscience he thought he would tell the truth'. He then related a long history of casual sexual, one-off encounters with various men; he rarely knew their names. He also confessed to a relationship with a cowherd named Loup with whom he had slept and had sex on many occasions. The sorcery played no part in the sodomy trial and was eventually dropped from the case. As with some of the trials above, it is clear that a fair number of men had been the objects of his assaults but had made no complaint to the court. He made no mention of sex with a woman and his confession appears to have been spontaneous. Also, his history implies that it was relatively easy and common for men to make sexual advances on one another and, as often as not, to have them reciprocated. In an age in which sodomy could lead to death (as it did here; Louis was burned), the casual nature of Louis' sexual encounters is insightful.

The availability of sex as well as the apparent willingness of people to look the other way is highlighted in the next case. In 1647, the Genevan authorities arrested Genaro Majone (from Naples, aged thirty-five) and his wife, Marguerite Medissa (from Milan, aged thirty-three), as well as Jean Farina (from Verona, aged thirty-six) and Farina's valet, Thaddeus Marturey (from the Ticino, aged twenty). The case appears to have begun when the group, who were travelling together, were suspected of various thefts in Lausanne and Geneva. The court was particularly interested in the close relationship among the group and the fact that they pooled their resources despite claiming that they were accidental companions. The two men had been mercenaries and the three Italians had travelled widely together throughout France, Switzerland and Germany.

Farina, when questioned about the thefts and the group's travel arrangements, spontaneously confessed to having had sex with his valet. It would appear that he may have done so because he did not completely understand what was going on in the trial. At various stages in the case Italian-speakers were brought in to ensure that both the judges and the defendant understood one another. Although he had a wife and children, he admitted that he had had sex with Thaddeus.

For his part, the valet also freely confessed, saying he had submitted to mutual masturbation, intercrural sex and buggery (but not oral sex) because he was afraid of being beaten or losing his job. A very young Burgundian servant was also involved. The latter seems to have been freed on account of his age as he does not appear in the trial. Three medical practitioners examined Thaddeus, the Burgundian, and Farina. The two servants were found to have been buggered rather forcefully but not Farina (he had taken only the active role). Although the court assumed that Majone and his wife knew about the buggery they could not prove it, and released them then banished them on pain of death. Farina was tied to a stake, strangled and then burnt 'until his body was reduced to ashes'. Thaddeus, being younger and having been solicited, was simply hanged.

The most interesting case from seventeenth-century Geneva revolved around Pierre Canal. These trials are fascinating in revealing one of the earliest 'networks' of sodomites north of the Alps. In addition, the wide range of social backgrounds, civic statuses and professions involved is fascinating. Just as importantly, the size of this group of sodomites in a city which probably had only 12,000 inhabitants is simply amazing. Geneva's fame for the effectiveness of its surveillance systems (elders, ministers, watch captains, etc.) would seem to imply that such a large-scale 'underclass' or 'subculture' could not exist. Nevertheless, it did.

On 12 January 1610, the city arrested Pierre Canal as a Savoyard spy. Eight years before Savoyard forces had almost overwhelmed the city in a surprise attack (the still celebrated *Escalade*). Geneva's independence, gained in the 1530s, remained precarious and the discovery of a spy in the midst of the city was spectacular news. What was even more surprising and dangerous was Canal's place in Genevan society. Not only was he a citizen but he was the Senate's factor or steward, the city's *Saultier*. Thus, he had access to every state secret.

In an effort to identify the scale of the spying, the city placed Canal's life under close scrutiny. They had no trouble uncovering his relationship with various Savoyards, especially Mon. de Montfalçon as there were incriminating letters. However, the various depositions taken all remarked on his notoriety as a sodomite. Any number of people knew he had had sex with men. There were even reports from Zurich that he had been in trouble there for relations with older teenagers. However, Zurich had not pursued the case as they did not want to cause a diplomatic incident. During numerous interrogations, including those in which torture was employed, Canal confessed and named a surprising number of people. He admitted to having paid for sex and having been paid, though his social position would imply that he did not need the money. He also suggested a lively trade in older students at the academy and college. Finally, to the shock of the judges he admitted not only to passive and active buggery but also to oral sex.

NAME (AGE)	STATUS & JOB	CONFESSED TO...	SENTENCE	DATE
Jean Buffet (23)	Habitant, tailor	Fornication with whores, indecent talk with Canal	Banished	1610
Claude Bodet (45-50)	Bourgeois, baker	Frottage, intercrural sex, mutual masturbation, oral sex	1,000 écus fine	1602
Antoine Artaud (30)	Wool carder, soldier	Mutual masturbation, oral sex without ejaculation	Banished	1608

NAME (AGE)	STATUS & JOB	CONFESSED TO...	SENTENCE	DATE
Jean Bedeville (23)	Habitant	Mutual masturbation, oral sex without ejaculation	Banished	1605
Paul André (23)	Tailor	Male prostitution, mutual masturbation		1609
Noel Destalle (25)	Baker	Oral sex, mutual masturbation, frottage		1603
Mathieu Bergeron (36)	Citizen, printer	Fondling	Banished	1604
Abel Bonniot (20)	Soldier	Oral sex without ejaculation	Drowned	
François Felisat (24)	Native, carder	Frottage, oral sex	Drowned	
Pierre Gaudy (18)	Citizen, surgeon	Oral sex without ejaculation	Drowned	1610
George Plonjon, Lord Bellerive (25)	Citizen	Fondling	Sacked from council posts	
Jean Maillet (61)	Citizen	Nothing	Released	

Although most of the cases involved the use of torture, the information uncovered was fairly consistent and presents the picture of a network of individuals (see the accompanying table) introduced to one another through contact with Canal.

The court was amazed not only by the social mix of the group but also by their frequent social visits to one another's homes and the number of times they spent the night with each other. The table gives some idea of the extent of this group as well as the length of time Canal had been practising his particular interest in oral sex (the final column notes the date the relationship began). What these trials show is the extensive nature of the subculture in Geneva. Many of the men were married but they were still willing to be involved in an activity (oral sex) which deeply shocked the Genevan magistrates. The cases also strongly imply that there must have been areas known to be 'safe' for meeting people and some system whereby an individual could 'pick-up' someone. The other trials, indeed, suggest that a low level of sexually explicit and suggestive talk and action (especially in shared beds) was tolerated and probably made it much easier for individuals of shared interests to meet one another.

While this case is interesting it is important to remember that sodomy cases simply disappear from the Genevan criminal records in the mid-seventeenth century and do not re-appear for nearly a century. At the moment there is no adequate explanation for this. For the purposes of this discussion, though, it does allow us to move rather quickly to an examination of the eighteenth century by which time, or so it has been argued for major metropoles such as London and Paris, attitudes had changed and an 'image' and stereotype of a sodomite had come into common parlance.

This new image is obvious almost from the beginning of the century. In 1703, Thomas Baker, in *Turbridge-Walks* had the foppish, male character Maiden say:

When I was at School… I lov'd mightily to play with Girls, and dress Babies, and all my Acquaintance now never quarell'd in their lives… Oh! The best Creatures in the World; we have such Diversion, when we meet together at my Chambers. There's Beau *Simper*, Beau *Rabbitsface*, Beau *Eithersex*, Colonel *Coachpole*, and Count *Drivel* that sits with his Mouth open, the prettiest Company at a bowl of Virgin-Punch; we never make it with Rum nor Brandy – like your Sea Captains, but two Quarts of Mead to half a pint of White Wine, Lemon-Juice, Burridge, and a little Perfume. Then we never read Gazets… like you Coffee-House Fellows; but play with Fans, and mimick Women, *Skream, hold up your tails, make Curtsies*, and *call one another, Madame.*

As well as,

Why, I can Sing, and Dance, and play upon the Guitar, make Wax-Work, and Fillagree, and Paint upon Glass. Besides I can dress a Lady up a Head upon Occasion, for I was put Prentice to a Milliner once, only a Gentleman took a fancy to me, and left me an Estate; but that's no Novelty, for abundance of People now-a-days take a fancy to a handsome Young Fellow… [Though] I can Raffle with the Ladies, Dance with them, and Walk with 'em in publick, I never desire any private Love-favours from 'em.

Baker is also assumed to be the author of *The Female Tatler* (1709) which mentioned a fashion boutique in Ludgate Hill. A noble customer noted that the shop assistants were the 'sweetest, fairest, nicest, dish'd out [male] Creatures; and by their Elegant Address and Soft Speeches, you would guess them to be Italians' while the three owners who sold their 'Gay Fancies' were 'positively the greatest fops in the Kingdom'. With an increasing emphasis on public morality and greater state control of the stage it became more difficult to portray sodomy (especially, paederasty) openly even to ridicule it as this smacked of 'promoting' the vice (rather as any discussion of homosexuality became impossible with laws against 'promoting it in schools'). Thus, the effeminate character became a code for the sodomite much as Mr Humphreys in *Are You Being Served*.

Moreover, the situation became very complicated for actors as well as their characterisations. They now had to ensure no hint of 'unnatural' passions was attached to them. In the late seventeenth and early eighteenth centuries association with libertine interests was not a disability (as we have noted above). For example, the assumptions underlying the scurrilous attacks on the actor James Noakes in a *Satyr on the Players* seems not to have harmed him.

> You smockfac'd Lads, Secure your Gentle Bums
> For full of Lust and Fury See he comes!
> 'Tis B[ugger] *Nokes*, whose unwieldly [Tarse]
> Weeps to be buryed in his Foreman's [Arse]
> Unnatural Sinner, Lecher without Sense,
> To leave kind [cunt], to live in Excrement.

Nor was actor and playwright John Leigh harmed by a reputation that was later mentioned by William Chetwood, in *A General History of the Stage* (1749), as a man of 'particular amiable Form, and genteel Address... [who] might have been in the good Graces of the Fair-Sex, if his taste had led him that way'.

However, by the latter half of the century, the situation had changed dramatically. Bickerstaff, the close friend and collaborator of Garrick, was accused of making advances on a soldier. He fled for France and was ruined. So terrified was Garrick of any of the scandal touching him that he repudiated his friend and refused any further contact with him. One attempt to defend Garrick's *volte-face* said:

> You rail at *Bick[erstaff]* with all my heart:
> Think you I mean to take *his* part?
> Think you I would one distich write
> T'exculpate a vile s[odomit]e?
> No, on him let thy rage be hurl'd;
> No, – lash him naked thro' the world:
> Expose in satire's keenest lays
> This skulking, dam'd detested race.
> Hang up to publick scorn each brute
> Who dares Love's rite to prostitute.

So complete was Bickerstaff's disgrace that is it not known where or even when he died.

The image of the effeminate sodomite moved from the stage to the streets. However, the problem was that the image did not accord with reality despite the apparent best efforts of both the 'sodomites' and their villifiers. *The World* (1754) complained about 'these louts of six feet high, with the shoulders of porters and the legs of chairmen, [who] affect "to lisp, and to amble, and to nick name God's creatures"'. Nathanial Lancaster, in *The Pretty Gentleman* (1747) presented the stereotype clearly,

Observe that fine Complexion! Examine that smooth, the Velvety skin! View that *Pallor* which spreads itself over his Countenance! Hark, with what a feminine Softness his Accents steal their Way through his half-opened Lips! Feel that soft Palm!... The whole System is of a finer Turn, and superior Accuracy of Fabric, insomuch that it looks as if Nature had been in doubt, to which Sex she should assign *him*.

Or, Garrick's description,

> A *man*, it seems – 'tis hard to say –
> A *woman* then? – a moment pray; –
> Unknown as yet by sex or feature,
> Suppose we try to guess the creature;
> Whether a *wit*, or a *pretender*?
> Of *masculine* or *female* gender?

While this characterisation is apparent and very decidedly a feature of the eighteenth-century English stage one cannot be sure that it dates wholly from the period. For example, one might contrast these stereotypes with that implied by Lestoile in his journal (1576) when he discussed the *mignons* or favourites of Henry III of France.

The name of the Mignons began, at this time, to travel by word of mouth among the people, to whom they were very odious, as much for their make-up, and effeminate and immodest apparel, but above all for the immense and liberal gifts presented them by the King... These handsome Mignons wore their hair a bit long, curled and recurled by cunning workmanship, on top of which they wore little velvet bonnets, as whores of the brothel do. The ruffs of their cloth shirts are of starched finery and one half foot long, so that their heads look like St John's on the platter. The rest of their clothing is similar.

Nevertheless, the sodomites seemed to have taken to the image in the eighteenth century at all social levels as one can hear in an overheard exchange between two mollies, 'where have you been saucy Queen? If I catch you strolling or cater-wauling, I'll beat the milk out of your breast I will so.'

This comment returns us to practice from theory and stage. In 1726 a raid on mollie-houses in London resulted in twenty places being discovered. The most famous was that of Margaret 'Mother' Clap. She was pilloried as a result – so badly that she fell off the pillory and fainted twice. It was during this period that sodomites were often seriously bruised or even blinded when in the pillory as a result of the dung (piled high in carts near at hand for the purpose) hurled by the crowd. Although the environment was changing the behaviour continued as the tour guide to St Paul's whisper-ing galleries discovered when (in 1731) he chanced upon William Hollywell buggering William Higgins in the upper part of the cathedral.

Nor should one suppose that this sort of change in state interest was confined to England or London. In Paris as well, the authorities were increasingly interested in controlling the sexual activities of the sodomites, or paederasts. However, they were more concerned about limiting acts of indecency in public than in actual prosecutions. Thus, they conducted patrols in well-known 'cruising' areas and kept copious records on any individuals suspected of 'unnatural' interests. The result is a fascinating amount of information on how men managed to find men in public places and how they then negotiated their particular desires.

In 1724, one man was approached by another. Both were clearly interested in sex but when the first man offered the other money for the encounter the second man huffily replied that 'he was not doing it out of interest... but only for his pleasure'. Another gentleman complained that 'as I was about to [piss], [he] asked me what time it was according to my cock and said that according to his it was high noon'. A later account, in 1737, noted that four men had been discussing their sexual exploits so loudly as they crossed the Pont-Neuf that passers-by had upbraided them for their indecency. Also, as one male prostitute made clear, the aversion to oral sex noticed a century earlier in Geneva had somewhat lessened: 'I perform the act with my mouth, in the same way as with my ass when I see that a man is clean and doesn't smell of women.'

Clearly, these men were understood by others and themselves as being a category rather apart. As the Marquis de Sade put it in a comment that also called for a more tolerant attitude and explicitly rejected the 'unnatural' charge levelled against sodomy: 'is it not clear that this is a class of men different from the other, but also created by nature?' Even the Paris paederasts were more than able to identify one another. The police records report overhearing two men, upon seeing another suspected sodomite, saying, 'there's somebody who looks like one. Let's split up and see what this sister is all about' and when another boy failed to respond to their banter at all 'they said to each other, "let's let him go, he doesn't speak Latin"'.

Moreover, many of these men not only clearly articulated their preferences but also demonstrated an acceptance of the prevailing view that relationships should be based on affection. Thus Gallimard, a lawyer of the Paris *parlement* reported that he 'had a wife but hardly ever made use of her, that his marriage was a stratagem, cover-up, and that he had not a taste for women, that he preferred an ass to a cunt'. Reporting on another sodomitical relationship, an officer noted that:

> Dusquenel and Dumaine had been sleeping together for two years. They were unable to fall asleep without having mutually touched each other and without having performed infamous acts. It was even almost always necessary for Dusquenel to have his arm extended along the headboard, under Dumaine's head. Without that Dumaine could not rest.

It may only be the survival of specific types of sources that have allowed us this sort of insight into the personal relationships and views of these men. However, some of the earlier cases, especially from Geneva, suggest that some relationships even then were long-standing and may well have involved deep feelings of mutual affection. All the more so as the maintenance of a sodomitical relationship (rather than one-night stands) under the threat of stake or gallows implies an amazing level of commitment.

Two rather detailed cases from eighteenth-century Geneva suggest some similar changes in attitude. In 1787, in one of the first cases since the mid-seventeenth century, the city's investigating magistrate was asked to examine the behaviour of Jacob Ponçon. The case revolved around accusations that

Jacob had approached some of the city's soldiers and asked for sex. However, it was a bit more complex in that Jacob's wife suggested that the soldiers were actually trying to blackmail her husband, as they had the previous year, but this time he had refused to pay. Indeed, a number of soldiers testified that Ponçon had attacked them physically when they admitted that they knew and were friends with Claude le Brun (aged twenty-seven), a grenadier of the Republican regiment who was the chief witness against Ponçon.

However, further investigations uncovered a number of other soldiers to whom advances had been made by Ponçon. Bertholomy Come (aged twenty-two) said they had struck up a conversation one evening while he was on patrol behind the hôtel-de-ville above the city walls. Ponçon had noted that the problem with sentry duty was the lack of women. Further banter had revealed that Come had too little money to attract the girls and then Ponçon had suggested that he might be able to earn a little. At this point the penny had dropped for Come and he told Ponçon to go away. He had also propositioned Henri Valotton (aged eighteen) who had told him 'I am not the man for you'. Likewise, he had been repulsed by Etienne Bovet (aged twenty-one) and, thereafter, whenever they met Ponçon 'turned very red'. François de Meuret (aged thirty-two) told a similar story and noted that he had pointed out Ponçon to Bovet with a warning to be wary of him.

Although these soldiers all told of their rejection of Ponçon, civilians interviewed in the case told a different story. Jean-Henri Valette (aged thirty-seven) said he had gone to Ponçon's private garret (which he maintained separately from his lodgings with his wife) because two soldiers had been seen going in. Saying he had something to sell he walked straight into the room. One of the soldiers jumped away from Ponçon but the other one was nowhere to be seen. Ponçon, on the other hand, was standing behind a sheet and appeared to be totally nude though Valette could only see him from the waist up. Ponçon said he was getting a clean shirt and would be with him soon. About fifteen minutes later one soldier, followed shortly thereafter by another, came downstairs and left. Then Ponçon arrived as though nothing untoward had happened. He also said that Ponçon's wife had told him they had not had sex in over seven years and that, in Lyon, he had always been in the company of a known sodomite.

Clearly, Ponçon's tastes were widely known and had not been too much of a problem until the 'relationship' with the soldier Le Brun had soured. The most interesting testimony in the case comes, though, from Ponçon's surgeon, Louis Jurine (aged thirty-six). When asked, he related that he had been treating Ponçon, since at least 1780, for a number of ailments that he thought linked to anal intercourse. He had strongly advised Ponçon to change his habits or that he would suffer serious medical problems. Also, he had tried to break his professional connection with Ponçon (though he made no effort to report him to the authorities) because he was so disgusted. However, he had relented at the supplication of Ponçon's physician, Mon. Menadier.

The case was troubling for the prosecuting magistrate who thought it potentially very embarrassing for the city. He noted, in his recommendation to the court, that the city had not had a prosecution for a century and that in most legal books and histories the punishment for the crime was death. Also, he said there were pragmatic reasons for taking a harsh line – the city was garrisoned by a thousand single men some of whom had already been debauched. However, he implied that a death sentence would cause some trouble as well and suggested that Ponçon (who had already fled the city) should be banished, *in absentia*, on pain of death and his estate heavily fined.

Two years later, in 1789 on the eve of the French Revolution, the city's government dealt with the public condemnation (at an open meeting of the Senate) of Jacques Dombres (aged forty) who ran a billiard hall frequented by many young men. A few of the men who were habitués of the establishment complained that Dombres had frequently touched their bottoms and genitals. He often commented on the 'loveliness of their asses' and had even fondled himself in their presence under the pretext of warming himself by the fire. David Levrier said he had been going to the place for about a year before anything happened and then Dombres had started touching him and saying, 'what a lovely ass, what a lovely ass it's nice and big', as well as other things 'not fit to repeat'. Apparently, Dombres had a penchant for big arses; perhaps the objects of his advances were offended as much by his comments as their intent.

To the consternation of the city, Dombres was convinced by a number of his other patrons that he should respond to the accusation by suing for slander (*à la* Oscar Wilde). Initially, he had not taken the situation seriously but they had told him that such a charge could not go unanswered. Indeed, his first response was to laugh and say that if he were so inclined 'he would not have had to have been treated for the disease one gets from women'. Once he brought a suit, though, the magistracy was forced to look into the case. His young supporters were his undoing. They all reported that he did touch bottoms and comment on their size and attractiveness. However, they argued that this was meaningless for two reasons. First, he said and did the same thing with regard to women's bottoms. Secondly, no one took him seriously and it was all a big joke. The city's fathers failed to see the humour of the situation. Dombres' supporters also implied that the men had never complained before and they were doing this out of spite because of a dispute. Again, this hardly endeared Dombres to the court. Eventually though they were inclined to consider the case a relatively mild matter. He was admonished and told he would have to find another profession; they closed his billiard hall.

It is clear that, over time, there was a marked shift in attitudes to some varieties of sodomitical behaviour between men. Increasingly, men who had sex with other men were seen as men wholly attracted to other men. Practical bisexuality, which seems to have been fairly common in the earlier part of our period, became less so – or, at least, was thought to be less common. However, the lack of a clear stereotype cannot be assumed. Geneva's judges showed a consistent assumption that a man was more likely to be guilty of sodomy if he had never had sex with a woman. Defendants were aware of the same 'image' and often advanced their previous sexual dalliances with women in their own defence.

Also, the description of Henry III's *mignons* reminds one of the danger of relying too heavily on the literary and criminal records of a single country. Even with the greater socio-cultural acceptance of a stereotype of the effeminate sodomite (be he a molly in England or a paederast in France) any number of sources comment with confusion and annoyance on the failure of convicted sodomites to match the model. In particular, the involvement of married men was a source of consternation. It seems wholly appropriate to end this chapter with a quotation from a forty-three-year-old upholsterer at the gallows. This married father of two had been convicted of sodomy and as he looked out over the crowd and almost certainly his family he articulated an emotional complexity that belies the historian's attempts to pigeonhole 'sodomites' into historical and cultural stereotypes: 'both of [my children] behave mightily well, and to the satisfaction of all concerned with them: and [I hope] that the world [will] not be so unjust as to upbraid [my] poor children with [my] unfortunate death'.

six

CHILD ABUSE
AND PAEDERASTY

In modern society, there are few crimes held in greater abhorrence than the sexual abuse of children. This disgust at the destruction of childhood's innocence and the inflicting of pain and trauma on the young was also a feature of earlier societies. Lawyers and judges frequently commented on the loss of innocence as well as their surprise that the assailant did not stop when it was obvious that the victim (a child) was in pain. Time and again it seemed incredible to these officials and dignitaries that anyone would continue to cause physical and emotional distress for no other reason than the fulfillment of 'base and beastly appetites'.

Although the visceral reaction of officials and parents in these societies is similar to ours there are important differences. First, modern societies have distinct ages of legal maturity for sexual activities. In most, one minute before midnight of the sixteenth birthday (or fourteenth, or eighteenth) the individual is a child afforded the full and potent protection of the law. A minute later, the individual is an adult almost wholly abandoned by the law. Females often pass into 'legal' adulthood at a younger age and some societies attempt to protect even those who are 'legally' of age from predation from authority figures (such as teachers). The important point is that modern nations have clear and specific 'ages of consent' for sex, marriage, drink, the vote, driving, and service in the armed forces. Quite often these ages vary dramatically from twelve to twenty-one. Thus, a person might be able to marry at fourteen but only drink at twenty-one (if at all).

The situation in the world before the French Revolution was substantially different in the area of legal maturity. Most societies had an age at which a person became free of parental control and able to exercise full civic rights. Usually, this was around twenty-five years of age. Depending on one's profession, this might also be the age at which one could marry under guild restrictions. However, the emphasis was upon one's ability to enter into legal contracts as an independent individual. What these societies never really tried to do was to define with legal precision the exact moment at which a child became a sexual adult. Indeed, this twofold understanding of development would not have been understood.

Jean Calvin, the famous Protestant reformer and a trained lawyer, was once asked to give advice on the correct way to deal with five schoolboys who had been caught fooling around with one another. He and his fellow lawyers said that there were three stages of sexual development and maturity. The earliest and first stage (childhood) was the period in which a person did not understand sexual activity and could not perform sexually. That is, the child was immature both physically and psychologically. In the next stage (adolescence)

134

the person was able sexually to perform but lacked a clear understanding of the enormity of their actions. Or, as Roger Edgeworth preached in the 1550s, adolescents 'although neither children in age, neither in condition, [are] all given to take their pleasures, and to follow their lusts'. Thus, being unmarried, an adolescent was in danger of committing a range of sins (fornication, adultery, sodomy, bestiality) without full comprehension. In the last stage of growing up (adulthood), the person was both physically and psychologically able to engage in sexual activities fully aware (by their conscience and the teachings of church and state) of the consequences of their actions.

These lawyers and theologians advised that children could not be held accountable for their part in a sexual act; they were purely victims of rape and abuse. Adolescents on the other hand could only be judged on the basis of the specifics of the case. They might be innocent, partially guilty, or entirely involved in the acts in a voluntary manner. Depending on the actual events an adolescent might be acquitted or executed (or given any range of punishments in between). An adult was fully accountable (unless mentally disturbed) and therefore liable to the full weight of the law.

This threefold understanding of physical, sexual, and psychological development is crucial for understanding the behaviour of individuals and societies in the cases about to be discussed. However, to complicate this situation, there was also the problem about the age of consent. Any given individual in any given trial might be placed on a different part of the continuum (child, adolescent or adult). Finally, there were also three general yet ill-defined types of 'criminal': the child abuser (sodomite or rapist depending on the gender of

the victim); the paederast (usually a twenty-something sexually involved with a teenager); and a sodomite (generally,
anyone committing an 'unnatural' act, specifically, two adult
males having [anal] sex).

So, when considering the reaction to sexual activities
involving anyone under the age of twenty (or so) one has to
remember that a category existed that does not exist today
and that there was no pre-conceived, exact age at which one
moved from one stage to the next. Also, that the law was not
entirely clear as to what crime was being committed. Hence,
the abuse of a male child was normally 'sodomy' while that
of a female child was 'rape'. Clearly, this made the task of the
judges much more difficult. It also meant, for example, that
one sixteen year old might be seen as an innocent victim
while another might be burnt at the stake.

The response of the law to the abuse of a child (as opposed
to an adolescent) was relatively straightforward – once the
crime was proven. The abuser (or rapist) was executed. The
difficulty then, as now, was the taking of evidence. This was
even more difficult in an age that lacked DNA testing or any
precise forensic science. Also, most of these crimes, by their
very nature, involved only a single adult and a child. Thus, the
burden of proof fell heavily on the child. Modern societies
struggle daily with the need to balance the sensitivities of a
traumatised child with the rights of the defendant. These same
concerns beset judges, lawyers, parents, and society more
generally from the Renaissance to the Enlightenment.

Despite these many concerns, dealing with the abuse of
children (as opposed to dispensing justice in cases involving
adolescents) was relatively easy. Three Geneva cases not only
demonstrate the visceral reaction to child abuse but also

introduce some of the complexities that even these cases occasioned. In 1577, Jean Genouillat was tried for raping a seven-year-old girl. In the course of the trial and under torture, he confessed to having raped a ten-year-old girl eighteen months previously and having engaged in sodomitical acts with boys. Initially he denied everything until he was confronted by the girl, Marie Besson, who detailed a string of five separate attacks over the course of a month. Jean had fondled her and engaged in frottage with her in front of her two younger siblings (Elisabeth and Paul). When questioned, Marie said she was 'very sore and [speaking quietly] she had trouble pissing'. With this testimony and that of Marie's mother, her siblings, various neighbours, and others whom Jean had indecently approached, he was tortured. As a result he confessed and was drowned for his crimes. None of the children involved was prosecuted.

However, it is clear that the context of even so straightforward a case was disturbing. Jean had lived in various homes in Geneva for four years. Gabrielle Ramiel testified that she had become concerned about the growing attachment between Jean and a certain stable-boy named Pierre and had warned Pierre to avoid Jean lest he get in trouble. Pernette Gernier told how she had seen him trying to share a bed with a boy of eleven in her home and that he had tried to crawl into her daughter's bed. When this happened, she had charged into the room, candle in hand, and said, 'Hey, sinner, is this the sort of thing you think you can do in my house?' Jaquema Martiod, a servant of Antoine Degallion, had caught Jean saying obscene things to Degallion's young daughter. She had told her master and he had beat Jean out of his house with a rod. In other words, a significant number of people knew (or suspected) that Jean was a danger to children but did nothing more than move him on. Clearly, they did not want to involve themselves or their young children in a trial. The difficulty Marie experienced in testifying (face-to-face with Jean, in the company of her mother, before a panel of over a dozen senior male magistrate judges) must have been a terrifying reality in the back of many a parent's mind.

Abel Revery, aged seven, underwent the same process when he accused Mathieu Durand of raping him in 1555. Unlike Marie, he went to his father and uncle immediately to report the attack by Mathieu, who was an apprentice printer living in his father's house. Marie's assault had come to public attention when her grandmother heard her talking to a young friend. She had been told by her attacker that she would get in trouble if she told anyone and she asked her friend if this were true. Mathieu, rather than threatening Abel, had tried to bribe him with money and the offer of a pet bird. Abel was required to testify a number of times and seems to have done so with little difficulty. He was examined by two barber-surgeons who swore that he had been forced. Mathieu admitted most of the details of the attack and, under torture, admitted the rape. He was executed for having:

> abandoned his person to a disgusting and beastly desire and appetite to commit and perpetrate the execrable crime of sodomy and in committing this desire and sinful appetite he had used and employed force to this end against the person of a young infant of a tender age.

The final case reminds the reader that the abuse of children was not entirely a male activity. In 1565, Thevena l'Heretier was arrested for abusing an eight-year-old boy. She immediately and freely admitted that she had previously fornicated in a rural village and that she had abused 'a young boy of tender and gentle age to accomplish her villainy and desire'. Her mistress, Perrine de Culliez, had two children with whom Thevena shared a bed. She loved them both but 'one wet the bed'. Until she was confronted by the older son, Vrie, she denied the accusations. She broke upon hearing his testimony. She confessed that she had fondled him, got on top of him, placed his penis against her privates and engaged in such violent frottage that he had been hurt. Jehan Cherubim, surgeon, confirmed that the child's penis was injured. Colladon, the legal advisor, said that he was 'injured in his penis, his little member, which clearly demonstrated how much force she had used and for how long [the attack] had continued'. The child's age made this a crime 'against nature' and 'she had given the said young boy [ideas] to do worse when he will be older'. Nevertheless, no penetration had taken place and it was not clear that the law had a definite idea of what crime had taken place. He advised, and the court agreed, that she should be flogged and perpetually banished.

In these cases, despite some difficulties, the children were more than able to testify against their attackers in front of a large gathering of adults. The fury of the parents at the attacks is apparent. The shock of the judges, lawyers and doctors is palpable. However, just as obvious is the desire of other parents to deal with the problem of a paedophile predator quietly and privately. It is also worth recalling that these societies had limited privacy. Children shared rooms (if not beds) with their parents or lodgers. Even urban dwellers would see animal sexual activity regularly. Moreover, traditional practice

pre-supposed a level of intimacy which would be unacceptable today. For example, in 1760, André Tissot (a physician
from Lausanne) wrote a treatise on the evils of masturbation.
He also had to attack strenuously the practice of parents and
nurses of fondling and masturbating young children to get
them to sleep. Nevertheless, in these Genevan cases, the
evidence was so overwhelming that a guilty verdict and execution was inevitable. However, this was not always the case.

Although sodomy was a capital offence in the British navy,
the case of Henry Brick gives some idea of how difficult a
conviction could be. John Booth, aged twelve, accused Brick
of raping him one Saturday night: 'he came into my hammo-
coe when I was asleep and unbuttoned his breeches and put
his private parts into my arse four times in my hammacoe that
night (and twice [on other occasions] in this ship)'. Another
seaman, Edward Gamble, had seen Brick getting into the
hammock and had heard the boy cry out. In addition, Brick
had been previously punished for being caught drunk fondling
another cabin boy. Nevertheless, the inability of the court to
prove categorically that rape (i.e., penetration) had taken place
resulted in a case proven only 'in part'. Brick was given 500
lashes and discharged rather than being executed.

As interesting (and disturbing) as these trials are, the reality
is that most cases involving younger people fall into the category of paederasty rather than paedophilia. Not only was this
crime more frequent but it was also more problematic. With
no clear concept of an 'age of consent', courts were left
judging the merits of each case on an *ad hoc* basis to decide
to what extent the youth (adolescent) might actually be culpable. Moreover, they had to deal with those cases which wholly
involved adolescents (teenage sexual experimentation).

In 1624, the Genevan courts prosecuted André Bron and Jean Chaix, both aged about eleven, for having sex with one another. In the course of the trial it became clear that their experimentation had also involved Samuel Moyne (aged four). Both said the other initiated the sexual encounters and that they had not actually understood what they were doing. They were both beaten in front of the city's schoolchildren; Samuel was not punished at all, being an innocent victim. A similar case in 1672 involved Jacques Descles (aged eleven) and Jean-Pierre Caillati (aged ten) in mutual masturbation, frottage and attempted anal intercourse. They admitted that they knew what they were doing was a sin but that they had done it 'simply because they were curious'. They had been shown what to do by an older adolescent named Jean-Pierre Pacquet who could not be found. They, too, were beaten.

The more common crime involving adolescents was sexual relations between a teenager and an older male (usually in his twenties or thirties). Although most societies throughout this period considered this a crime it was not always punished harshly. In addition, cultural norms complicated the situation. The Renaissance re-introduced the West to the mores of the pagan classical world where paederasty was more widely accepted and even extolled in myth (for example, the tale of Ganymede, the youth taken by Zeus as lover and cup-bearer). Lords Stanhope, Shaftesbury and Rochester were known for their adoration of women and adolescent males. One writer noted that 'among the chief men in some of the colleges [of Oxford and Cambridge] sodomy is very usual and the master of one college has ruined several young handsome men in that way [and] that it is dangerous sending a young man that is beautiful to Oxford'. William Cowper recalled the prevalence of effeminate boys at Westminster and that an Eton master had been sacked for paederasty. The cultural acceptance of youth-love and the accompanying ambivalence was spectacularly articulated by William III who said, 'it seems to me a most extraordinary thing that one may not feel regard and affection for a young man without its being criminal'.

Social and cultural acceptance of paederasty, which would today be rejected outright or limited by a strict application of a legal age of consent, has historically been more widely accepted. For example, young Mayan nobles in colonial Mexico were introduced to nobility and adulthood through rituals with older, socially superior nobles in which they learned 'about blood and semen'. Likewise, this had been part of the culture underlying Athenian paederasty (so familiar to Westerners steeped in the classical revival of the Renaissance and Humanism). The vast cultural gulf that separates our day from these other cultures can be best seen in the reaction one has to a quotation from Aristophanes' play *The Birds* when a man met a friend of the same (adult) age:

> Well, this is a fine state of affairs, you damned desperado! You meet my [teenage] son just as he comes out of the gymnasium, all fresh from the bath, and you don't kiss him, you don't say a word to him, you don't hug him, you don't feel his balls! And you're supposed to be a friend of ours!

It is almost impossible to comprehend that this is a throwaway joke in a play. However, unless one understands this ambivalent attitude to sexual activity between adolescents and others (whether adolescent or adult) it is impossible to appreciate how complex the legal and cultural situation actually was.

Thomas Middleton's *Michaelmas Term* (1605) satirised paederasty openly and the use of adolescent males to play women in Elizabethan and Stuart plays must have played on this social ambivalence as well as the implied humorous acceptability of aspects of paederasty.

It explains how the eighteen-year-old Charles Fielding, the son of Lord Denbigh, in the 1700s could be blackmailed for sexual misconduct and protected successfully by his family. Also, Frederico Marquioni, goldsmith to the viceroy of Aragon, was banished for soliciting a seventeen year old during the Feast of St John in 1625 – seventeen people testified against him. Jean-Baptista Cocharino, aged thirty-eight, a Venetian trumpet-player, was arrested for sex with a teenager and indecent relations with another six. He used his music to seduce them. Likewise, Robert of Flamborough, confessor of the St-Victor abbey in Paris reported the following dialogue:

> *Priest:* Have you sinned with a man?
> *Penitent:* With many.
> *Priest:* Have you initiated any innocent
> persons into this sin?
> *Penitent:* Yes, three students and a subdeacon.

The prevalence of paederasty is only slightly less surprising than the uncomfortable response of societies to it.

Two Genevan cases set the problems inherent in these crimes into stark contrast. In 1568, Louis Guey (aged seventy-two) was beheaded for sexual relations with Beatrice George (aged thirteen). For four months, he had been abusing the young girl. She had received money from him and, bizarrely, lessons in sex education as he had explained that 'his seed' was what caused pregnancies. The case became complicated when the midwives, called in to examine Beatrice, reported that 'they had found her pure, without being corrupted'. This then meant that penetration had not taken place and, thus, there was a question as to whether a crime (as opposed to a sin) had actually been committed. This was no minor problem. In England, it was not until *Regina v. Wiseman* (1710) that a judge ruled for the first time that sodomy included anal intercourse with a woman.

The city's chief legal advisor was more certain: 'Because of his great age he [should] not be subject to the same temptations and follies as a young man and it is against nature to for him [to have] addressed himself in such a manner to a girl so much younger'. In addition, 'the spilling of his seed on the ground [followed by] a detestable discussion [about it]' was especially shocking. The lawyer, Colladon, strongly recommended that Guey be executed 'to purge the church [i.e., society] of the evil and scandal'. The judges agreed and sentenced him to be decapitated and exposed on the gibbet. The public verdict specifically mentioned the gross inequality in their ages.

However, this was not the end of the story. Beatrice was also convicted of sexual misconduct and sentenced to be beaten in public. Why? A number of the features of the relationship uncovered in the investigation disturbed the judges. First, she had not told of the abuse. Instead, the relationship only came to light when Michel Grandon reported that, one night, while sleeping in the same room as Guey, Beatrice had come into the room and climbed into the old man's bed. She had tried to initiate sexual activities but Guey, suspecting that Grandon was only pretending to be asleep, sent her away.

Finally, while being held for questioning, she had propositioned one of the guards in the jail. The lawyers and the
judges agreed that her behaviour spoke of initiative and intent
on her part. Thus, she was not an 'innocent victim'. Rather,
she was culpable, in part. However, because of her age they
decided she was not fully accountable and should not receive
the full punishment afforded by law.

The magistrates were also concerned about the situation in
the family home more generally. Guey apparently slept in a
bed that was normally in the room where Beatrice and her
younger sister shared another bed. Her parents testified that
they had seen no reason to worry about their lodger's character. However, Beatrice's mother did admit that her daughter had mentioned that the old man had once touched her
bottom. She had discussed this with her husband and he had
told Beatrice to let him know if it happened again. The
authorities were certain that the parents had been lax in their
oversight and even contemplated the possibility that they had
colluded in the abuse in order to keep the lodger's rent
coming in. Eventually, the parents were exonerated but not
without a stern verbal warning from the bench.

This case, in particular, highlights the complexity of a situation in which there was no clear age of consent. The respon-
sibilities of the parents were ill-defined. The accountability of
the young girl was open to interpretation. The type of crime
(without actual penetration, *à la* Clinton) committed was
unclear. The only point that was agreed was that the extreme
age gap made the relationship, regardless of other considera-
tions, worthy of a severe penalty. Guey should have known
better, should have controlled himself, should have been
beyond such lusts.

The case (in 1662) of Col. Alphonse Crotto (aged forty-three) of Lucca in Italy and Jean Chabaud (aged thirteen) from Languedoc falls more into the normative pattern of early modern paederasty. Crotto had hired the boy as a servant while passing through Languedoc. The boy had already travelled to Catalonia. They had journeyed together for about six weeks during which time Crotto had repeatedly sodomised the young Chabaud both in various inns (where they had shared beds) and on the road. They had passed through Montpellier, Avignon, Valence, Romans, Grenoble, Chambéry and come, eventually, to Geneva.

Again, this case was complex. Crotto freely admitted to 'sodomy' though later recanted saying that, being an Italian speaker, he had not really understood the implications of the confession. He swore all he had actually done was frottage and 'external nighttime pollutions', by which he seems to have meant that he had become sexually aroused in his sleep and had ejaculated on the youth during these 'wet dreams'. There is every reason to assume that Crotto was well enough educated to realise that many civil and canon lawyers did not consider such semi-waking acts to be sins let alone crimes. The lack of penetration was also a crucial consideration. Not until 1817 (in England) was a man convicted and sentenced to death for 'sodomising' a seven-year-old boy by forcing the child to fellate him – and he was acquitted on appeal.

However, Chabaud was clear that sex had taken place. The six doctors who examined the boy were unable to offer conclusive proof that penetration had taken place. This made a conviction less likely but not impossible. Forensic evidence was extremely problematic but when doctors could agree it often proved to be conclusive: in 1730, Gilbert Lawrence was hanged because a doctor testified categorically that he had forced a fourteen-year-old boy. Just as worrying to the judges, though, was the fact that Chabaud had continued to travel with Crotto even after the abuse had started. Indeed, they had only learned of the relationship when a Genevan innkeeper heard the boy weeping in his room and found that he was badly bruised from anal sex. The innkeeper (who was also a member of the city's militia) had arrested Crotto and carried the youth to a doctor because he was unable to walk.

As with the case of Beatrice, this case of paederasty proved problematic for the court. Once they were convinced of Crotto's guilt (by recourse to torture) they had no problem sentencing him to be hanged and his lifeless body to be burnt. However, they were not sure what to do with Chabaud. In the end they decided that he was as culpable as Beatrice in that he had not run away from Crotto in any of the towns they had passed through nor had he attempted to inform on him. Thus, he had 'colluded' in his abuse. Consequently, he had to be punished. Legal advice suggested that his age should be a mitigating factor and, therefore, he was only beaten on Crotto's still smouldering ashes.

These individual cases give some idea of the widespread cultural ambivalence about, if not acceptance of, paederasty. However, the best example comes from the end of our period with the 'paederasty patrols' in Paris of 1780–83. These were directed by commissioner Pierre-Louis Foucault and police inspector Louis-Henry Noël who oversaw the police's division of paederasty which held the names of about 40,000 known offenders (both adolescent and adult). This division was specifically interested in relations involving adolescents and adults – only six of the 'adults' dealt with were guilty of 'child abuse' and even these had also had sex with 'adolescents'. This was a move by the police to control (but not eradicate) paederasty not paedophilia.

On 10 November 1780 at 6 p.m. these two men and their officers undertook the first 'paederast patrol'. They were on the lookout for anyone 'attired in such a way as to be recognised by everyone as a paederast': frock coat, large tie, round hat, small hair knot, shoes with bows. The men and youths they cautioned or arrested came from every level of society. Two of their premier catches were the Marquis de St-Clément (who had picked up, for the second time, an unemployed eighteen year old) and Mathurin Dupuy, a priest, who was arrested 'cruising' the Luxembourg gardens in his ecclesiastical robes.

In addition to the individual cases which will be discussed in slightly greater detail below, these records are very useful in giving specific details on those cautioned and arrested during these patrols. The table below gives an idea of the information that can be gleaned specifically as it relates to the age-range of the offenders. Slightly over 40% of these men were under the age of twenty-four while nearly 80% were under the age of thirty-five (the age by which most men would have been married). This is not to imply that the activity was *in lieu* of sex with women. The investigators were clear that these men chose to engage in this activity. Despite this predilection, the police showed no sign of trying to stop the activity. Rather they wanted to know who was involved and to control its more notorious (i.e., visible) manifestations.

It is also clear that their awareness of a 'dress code' among the paederasts was not just professional knowledge. On

AGE	NUMBER OF MEN	%
15–19	37	15.5
20–24	59	24.8
25–29	43	18.1
30–34	49	20.6
35–39	21	8.8
40–44	15	6.3
45–49	6	2.5
50+	8	3.4

Ages of the 238 men cautioned and arrested by the Paederasty Patrols of Paris 1780–83.

11 October 1781, the divisional records noted that Joseph Prainguet was jeered and chased through the boulevards of Paris for 'his indecent and distinctive costume'. He was saved from the crowd and warned not to dress that way again. Apparently, he was protected by a 'powerful employer' but this could not save him the second time he came to the attention of the police; he was then prosecuted. The role of the powerful was so important and crucial that the lieutenant-general of the Paris police even opined that 'paederasty, in the long run, can only be a vice of great nobles'.

The specific cases uncovered continue to highlight the complex nature both of the paederasts and of those who attempted to control their behaviour. In general, the police were more inclined to caution the youths, though repeat offending resulted in arrest. For example, a fifteen year old named Prudhomme was prosecuted only after having been released two months earlier. Also, the question of culpability was more complex even for the adolescent. Jean-Marie Paris, a sixteen-year-old apprentice cook, was raped by two men while making a delivery. His brother laid a complaint with the division. The young Paris, however, was clearly traumatised and used the money the men had forced on him afterwards to pay for Masses to cleanse 'his crime'.

Other youths were equally confused about what they should and should not do. For example, Jean-Pierre Varin (aged twelve) and Baptiste Dauthier (aged fourteen) were sexually involved with Joseph Lafosse (aged thirty-three), a wealthy jeweller. He told both of the boys to say nothing to their mothers as they were doing nothing wrong. He also said they should not confess to their priest as the priest was probably a paederast as well. Finally, he gave them money to keep them quiet. In his case, his casuistry and bribery failed to silence the youths who turned him in. Another youth, sixteen-year-old Lormant, followed a different path. He had been a Carmelite novice and become sexually involved with a fellow adolescent novice. He had then seduced two older brothers of the order (aged twenty-one and twenty-two). Thereafter, he left the monastery before taking his final vows and became a rent boy on the Champs-Elysées. However, his tastes continued to run to the sacred and he had two regular clients who were abbots.

The conclusions arising from these Parisian cases simply echo those elsewhere across Europe in the period from the Renaissance to the Enlightenment. Although there was a fairly subtle understanding of human sexual development from child through pubescent teenager (adolescent) to adult, there were no set legal ages for responsibility or consent. Modern societies are finding that they must cope with similar complexities. By amending laws on ages of consent to include clauses relating to those in positions of authority and trust, they are trying to include some of the *ad hoc*, case-specific discretion consistently used by early modern courts. These earlier courts explicitly dealt with and accepted the sexuality of the pubescent. They acknowledged a period of development in which innocence and culpability overlapped. The tasks faced by these courts were further complicated by a cultural set of values that idolised youthful male beauty and placed great stress on friendship and romantic attachments to 'attractive' youths. These cases simply highlight how difficult it was to decide when a relationship had moved from friendship to love to the physical to abuse. The continuum was complex and murky.

However, on one point these societies were clear. The abuse of the prepubescent was a capital crime. Anyone charged with the abuse of a child was almost certainly going to be convicted and executed because of the use of torture. The cases of child abuse also highlight another difference between early modern societies and the present day. Most children seem to have told their parents or elders immediately if they were abused. The children seem to have had few problems testifying face-to-face against their abusers. Indeed, one of the most striking features of child abuse cases is how rarely (almost never) the abuser is able to convince the child that he or she will be thought ill of. Usually, bribes or threats of violence were used to maintain the child's silence. That these societies never thought their children might hesitate to report abuse is confirmed in the trials of adolescents. Those who were punished with their adult partners were usually considered culpable because they had not reported the abuse – as everyone clearly assumed they would. In their reaction to child abuse the early modern world seems very modern indeed. However, in its attitude to adolescent sexuality and its expectation that children will speak openly to adults about being abused this early world seems truly alien.

seven

TRIBADES AND FEMALE SEXUAL DEVIANCE

According to the old chestnut, British legal reforms of the nineteenth century did not include lesbianism in laws against deviant sexual acts because Queen Victoria could not contemplate that such behaviour could take place. Indeed, as we shall see, there was a tradition emerging in late eighteenth and early nineteenth century English legal thought that 'good girls' (that is, educated women of quality) could not possibly engage in such vile acts. However, the period we are examining was under no such illusions.

Nevertheless, a number of problems confronted societies, judges and individuals when attempting to deal with same-sex acts between women. First and foremost, it was not clear what crime (if any) was being committed. Sodomy, by its very definition involved, at least, penetration and, more usually, anal penetration. Secondly, a male-dominated society and its courts was not really *au fait* with what women got up to at home amongst themselves and their maids. Also, because of traditional religious, medical and 'psychological' views about women, there was a real fear that publicising information about this crime might simply lead women to experiment – by their very nature they were ruled by their bodies in general and their sexual organs in particular. The last thing any male wanted to do was give them ideas. Or as one writer around 1700 (Jean-Baptiste Thiers) opined: 'experience teaches us that often it is better not to explain in detail what is forbidden, in order not to suggest the possibility of doing it'.

One of the earliest codes to mention same-sex acts between women simply highlights the problems. In 1270, a French code, prescribed that a man 'who has been proved to be a sodomite must lose his testicles and if he does it a second time, he must lose his member, and if he does it a third time he must be burned'. The same code said that 'a woman who [has sex with another woman] shall lose her member each time and on the third must be burned'. The law makes no attempt to explain what exactly a woman must do to be a sodomite or precisely how she can lose her 'member' once, let alone twice. Even with this technical confusion in the letter of the law the spirit of the codes, the Bible, and social norms were more than able to lead to the drowning of a girl in Speyer (Germany) for sex with another woman in 1477.

The reality is that very few cases are known and most of these come from the eighteenth century. Some cases survive from earlier periods and there was certainly a growing concern in the seventeenth century about female sexual activity and women's increasing knowledge of the body and all things sexual through scientific and classical literature and, in particular, through novels and erotic writings.

The increasing availability of Greek and Roman writers in the Renaissance was facilitated by the spread of printing. Aristophanes' comedies, for example *Lysistrata*, with its ribald humour springing from the refusal of Athenian and Spartan women to have sex with their husbands (but not each other) until and unless they stopped fighting, could be read in original and in translations. For example, an original edition appeared in 1525 and there was a good French version in 1692. Juvenal's satires which lampooned Roman sexual perversions, including lesbianism, were available from as early as 1486 and Martial's epigrams (of a similar nature) from 1482. As more women were taught to read both vernacular and classical literature this world became increasingly open to them. It may also explain why the expansion of female literacy in the mid-eighteenth century coincided with the increasing censorship and bowdlerisation of these and other classical authors.

Nor should one underestimate the impact of these works, accustomed as we are to dismissing the classics as boring. A few examples will suffice. Peter Green's Penguin translation (1974) of Juvenal's sixth satire says:

> [Maura] and her dear friend Tullia pass by the
>   ancient altar
> Of Chastity? And what is Tullia whispering to her?
> Here, at night, they stagger out of their litters
> And relieve themselves, pissing in long hard bursts
> All over the Goddess's statue. Then, while the Moon
> Looks down on their motions, they take turns to
>   ride each other
> And finally go home.

A similar overt and easy sexuality is apparent in Stephen Halliwell's verse translation of Aristophanes' *Lysistrata* (1997):

Lysistrata: Warm greetings, Lampito, dear Spartan friend.
Sweetheart, you're looking simply ravishing.
What gorgeous skin – and, oh, those muscles of yours.
You could throttle a bull!

Lampito: By the Twins, I swear I could.
My exercise includes rump-stretching kicks.

Kalonike: I've never seen a finer pair of breasts.

Lampito: Stop feeling my flesh; I'm not for sacrifice!

Lysistrata: And what about this other girl – who's she?

Lampito: A Boiotian – and a fine one, by the Twins.
She's come for the meeting too.

Myrrhine: A true Boiotian! Her belly's as flat as any Boiotian plain.

Kalonike [peering]: And look at her little bush, how cutely trimmed.

Lysistrata: This other girl?

Lampito: A choice piece, by the Twins. Korinthian, what's more.

Kalonike: A real 'choice piece'!
That's all too clear in front as well as behind.

One of Martial's epigrams (book 1: 90) goes beyond the graphic in its depiction and mocking of lesbianism as Peter Howell's translation (1980) shows:

Since I never used to see you, Bassa, close to males, and since no rumour provided you with an adulterer, but a crowd of your own sex discharged every function around you, with no man coming anywhere near, I used to think you, I admit, a Lucretia: but you – shame on it, Bassa! –

were a fucker. You dare clash together twin cunts, and your
unnatural kind of love lyingly imitates [manliness].

The lasciviousness of this literature (almost wholly intended
to amuse and titillate a male audience) was increasingly available to literate women of the aristocratic and upper-middle
classes.

The early modern period also produced its own erotic and
pornographic literature. Again, the audience was mostly male
but women increasingly had access to these works. Moreover,
the erotica had a significant lesbian element. Indeed, the usual
format for this literature was to have an older woman 'explaining' sex to an adolescent girl (echoing the paederastic aspects
of male culture). For example, *A School for Girls* (1688, originally published in French as *L'Ecole des filles* in 1655) had
chapters entitled: 'A discussion of mounting & various ways
of riding, as well as others which can be imagined'; 'whether
a man or a woman derives most pleasure from intercourse';
'why it is wrong to toy with girls'. Nicolas Chorier's *Satyra
Sotadica* (1660) was widely distributed (in French as *Académie
des Dames* and in English as *A dialogue between a married lady
and a maid*). One small selection is enough to give the flavour
of the genre:

> *Tullia* [an older married woman]: How I should like ye
> would grant me the power of playing the role of [your
> betrothed]…
> *Ottavia* [Tullia's younger, engaged cousin]: I am well aware
> that no pleasure can accrue to thee from a maiden as I
> am, nor to me from thee either… I should like thou
> wert [my betrothed]. How gladly would I then lay

> before thee all the fineries of my person… thy garden
> is setting mine on fire.

Despite their constant protestations against lesbian love they repeatedly have sex and their orgasms are especially highlighted in the text. Other books were in a similar vein as their titles imply: *The Wandering Whore* (1642); *Venus in the Cloister; or, the Nun in her Smock* (1683); *The Whores Rhetoric* (1683). Indeed, erotic literature almost always included lesbian acts either involving prostitutes or, more bizarrely and amusingly, aristocratic women (as Tullia and Ottavia above).

Although these works were increasingly common and more socially acceptable with the general relaxation of morals during the Enlightenment, this situation did not continue. The period of the French Revolution and Napoleonic Wars produced a widespread conservative reaction across Europe. Just as the Reformation had brought to an end much of the social liberalism accompanying the Renaissance and classical Humanism, the Enlightenment became tainted with the excesses of the Revolution. No better example of the individual impact of this cultural shift can be found than in Mrs Keith of Ravelstone, an aged aunt of Sir Walter Scott. He related that she had decided to re-read Aphra Behn's fiction which had been a favourite of her youth. When asked for her impressions of the stories after so many years she said,

> Is it not a very odd thing that I, an old woman of eighty
> and upwards, sitting alone, feel myself ashamed to read a
> book which, sixty years ago, I have heard read aloud for the

amusement of large circles, consisting of the first and most creditable society of London?

This brief vignette serves as a cautionary note for all that follows. This discussion opened with the Renaissance, a period of relative openness, followed by the moralising of the Reformation and the liberalising of the Enlightenment. In the decades following, morality was to come full circle ushering in the conservatism which would culminate in the so-called 'Victorian values' lauded by many a modern politician. Anyone calling for a return to the values of the past might be shocked by the result if the response was an enthusiasm for Renaissance or Enlightenment values rather than those of the Reformation or nineteenth century.

While it is clear that literate men and (increasingly over time) women were able to read accounts of lesbian sexual acts, there were also women engaging in these same activities. The literature, though clearly meant to titillate and arouse (men), was also an expression of a reality that these early modern societies tried very hard to ignore. Lesbianism was more than a male fantasy. It was a reality for women and these women paid for expressing their desires with fines, the lash, and the gallows.

Sadly, little evidence remains of lesbian activities or reactions to it before the eighteenth century. However, three cases from Geneva give some insight into how society dealt with lesbian sexuality. In late 1557, the Genevan church court, the Consistory, referred a case to the city's criminal court. Jeanne-Marie Libernet, a widow, was accused of debauching two young girls. She had said 'evil and unrepeatable things which scandalised the two girls to whom they had been said'. She had got into bed with one of the girls, Charlotte Preudhomme, while the other (Charlotte's maid, Jehanne Sorent) stood at the bedside. While fondling Charlotte she had told them that 'when she had been with her lover and betrothed in Italy, he had had his evil way with her twice and that his "rod" had been as big as his arm'. She had also told them more about 'Italian buggery'. (Italy was notorious for turning people to sodomy and she had probably told them about being sodomised by her lover.) She also said that 'men stuck certain hot things in a woman's belly' and that 'women could do the same to one another'. Jeanne-Marie was tortured but continued to protest her innocence and the court quickly realised that some of her accusers were also involved in an inheritance dispute with her. Unable to uncover the exact details of the case the judges eventually banished her 'on pain of being beaten if she returned'.

Two years later, in 1559, a similar case was brought against Jaquema Gonet, a teenage servant, because of her relations with her employer's two children, Esther (aged fifteen) and Nicolas Bodineau (aged eight). On a number of occasions while sharing the children's bed she had engaged in sexual acts with both of them. Nicolas had mentioned this to his parents but they had not taken him seriously (which greatly disturbed the judges – Etienne and Ylaire, the parents, were vigorously questioned by the court). According to the children, Jaquema had used her wiles and erotic conversation to get Esther to commit 'abominable acts of sodomy and a sin against nature'. She had also convinced Esther to join her in molesting Nicolas, 'an act of fornication which was also against nature especially in view of the great youth of the said poor little child'. She had excited Esther by telling her how even boys could 'make their members long' and they had then got Nicolas erect. While this was going on, Jaquema had been 'placing her finger in [Esther's] "nature"'.

1 Albrecht Dürer, *A Knight and his Lover* (1493), illustrates the conventional pose of lovers as well as the jealousy of the knight at finding his love in the arms of another.

AN
ESSAY
UPON
IMPROVING and ADDING
TO THE
STRENGTH
OF
Great Britain and Ireland,
BY
FORNICATION,
JUSTIFYING
the same from *Scripture* and *Reason*.

By a Young CLERGYMAN.

Omne tulit punctum qui miscuit utile dulci. Hor.

Gen. Chap. i. v. 28. *And God blessed them, and said unto them, Be fruitful and multiply, and replenish the Earth.* Chap. ix. v. 1. *And God blessed Noah and his Sons, and said unto them, Be fruitful, and multiply, and replenish the Earth,* v. 7. *And you, be ye fruitful and multiply, bring forth abundantly in the Earth, and multiply therein.*

DUBLIN,
Re-printed in the Year M.CC.XXXV.

2 This work, extolling the virtues of fornication and essaying to prove its value through the Bible, scandalised polite society.

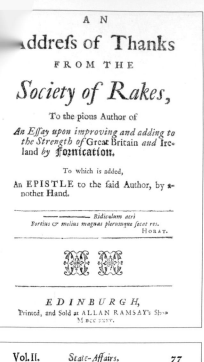

AN

ddrefs of Thanks

FROM THE

Society of Rakes,

To the pious Author of

*An Effay upon improving and adding to
the Strength of* Great Britain *and* Ireland *by* fornication.

To which is added,

An EPISTLE to the faid Author, by a-
nother Hand.

——————— *Ridiculum acri*
Fortius & melius magnas plerumque fecat res.
HORAT.

EDINBURGH,
Printed, and Sold at ALLAN RAMSAY's Shop
M DCC XXXV.

Vol. II.   *State-Affairs.*   77

F A B. XIII.

Of the other **Members** confpiring againft the
Belly.

ONce on a Time the Hands and Feet
   With Back, and Loins, and Bum, did meet
In a Rebellious Confult, where
The B——ch as Speaker took the Chair,
And with an uncouth hollow found
The following Treafon did propound :
Brethren, quoth he, you know the' Head
Makes us to toil and fweat for Bread,
Yet nothing to our Lot doth fall,
But *idle Gut* confumes it all.
My Friends, if you'l be rul'd by me,
We will fhake off this Tyranny.
If Head and Belly will have Meat,
Let them toil for't with Hands and Feet.
Agreed, fays Back, I vow and fwear,
For them I'll no more Burdens bear.
Content, fays Bum, if't be your Will ;
For I love dearly to fit ftill.
Says Feet, I'll no more Errands run.
The Loins fay, Brethren, it is done.'
The Hands vow they would work no more,
And wifh they'd been as wife before.
The Members thus in Holy League,
Did blefs themfelves for this Intrigue.
But fuddenly the Hands grew weak,
The Feet grew numb, the Loins did fhake,
The Back was feeble, the Bum grew poor,
And Breech the Chair-man loud did roar,
Pray cram the Gut, and we'll rebel no more.

F 2

This page, clockwise from top left:

3 Clearly, not every element in society
was scandalised by the suggestion that
fornication had positive value.

4 Detail from Mirabeau's *Ma
Conversion* (London, 1783) showing a
most imaginative and physically
demanding sexual position.

5 This poem purports to discuss the
effects of a rebellion of the body's
parts, led by the arse, against the mind.

Facing page:

6 This work and illustration 7 (a later
edition) attack the evils of murder and
adultery, which are linked together, while
extolling the virtues of friendship and
chastity.

The Glory
of
GOD'S REVENGE
against the
Bloody & detestable
Sins of
MURTHER
and
ADULTERY
exprest in 30 Trag:
Histories

To which are anex'd
the Triumphs of
Friendship & Chastity

By Tho: Wright,
M.A.

Printed for Benja.
Crayle
in Fleet Street.

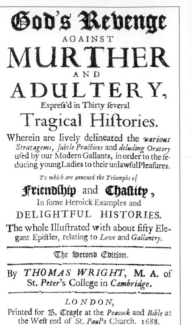

God's Revenge

AGAINST
MURTHER
AND
ADULTERY,

Expreſs'd in Thirty ſeveral
Tragical Hiſtories.

Wherein are lively delineated the *various*
Stratagems, ſubtle Practices and *deluding Oratory*
uſed by our Modern Gallants, in order to the ſe-
ducing young Ladies to their unlawful Pleaſures.

To which are annexed the Triumphs of
Friendſhip and Chaſtity,
In ſome Heroick Examples and
DELIGHTFUL HISTORIES.

The whole Illuſtrated with about fifty Elegant Epiſtles, relating to *Love* and *Gallantry*.

The Second Edition.

By *THOMAS WRIGHT*, M. A. of
St. *Peter*'s College in *Cambridge*.

LONDON,
Printed for B. Crayle at the *Peacock* and *Bible* at
the Weſt end of St. *Paul*'s Church. 1688.

ANE

DETECTIOVN
of the duinges of Marie
Quene of Scottes, touchand
the murder of hir huſband,
and hir conſpiracie, adulterie, and
pretenſed mariage with the Erle
Bothwell. And ane defence
of the trew Lordis, main-
teineris of the Kingis
graces actioun and
authoritie.

Tranſlatit out of the Latine
quhilke was written
by *G. B.*

Clockwise from top left:

7 Note the specific reference to 'modern
gallants [who seduce] young ladies to their
unlawful pleasures'.

8 Albrecht Dürer, *The Joys of the World* (pre-
1490), shows another example not only of
the conventional pose of lovers but also the
public acceptance of the embrace. Indeed,
the other characters are entirely indifferent.

9 This work particularly attacked Mary,
Queen of Scots, for her adulterous
relationship with the Earl Bothwell.

THE

Wandring whore

CONTINUED:

A DIALOGUE

BETWEEN
Magdalena a Crafty Bawd,
Julietta an Exquisite Whore,
Francion a Lascivious Gallant,
And *Gusman* a Pimping Hector.

Discovering their diabolical Practises at the
Half-crown CHUCK-OFFICE.

With an Additional LIST *of the names of the*
Crafty Bawds, Common Whores, Wanderers,
Pick-pockets, Night-walkers, Decoys,
Hectors, Pimps and Trappanners.

Delivered to the Publisher hereof by a late Hector, several
deep Pyemen, and decayed Gamesters amongst them.

John: 11. *Sine Cerere & Baccho friget Venus.*

London : Printed in the Year 1660.

Luc. 12.

10 The enthusiasm of the literate and theatre-going public for relatively explicit plays in the seventeenth century contrasts with the greater restraint and 'respectability' of the eighteenth-century stage.

11 The combination of a man being sodomised and a woman sodomising him (presumably with the aid of an artificial device) must have been shocking – and titillating – on almost every level imaginable.

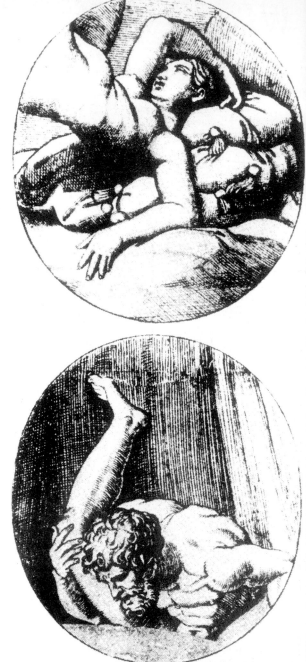

12 This detail from Marcantonio Raimondi, *Amori degli Dei* (1524), giving yet another sexual variation, highlights the access that the literate had to sexually explicit material at the very moment that Europe was about to be plunged into the Reformation.

13 The sexual positions shown here and in illustration 12 can be seen as one of the last expressions of the openness of the Renaissance before the moral crusades of the Protestant and Catholic Reformations.

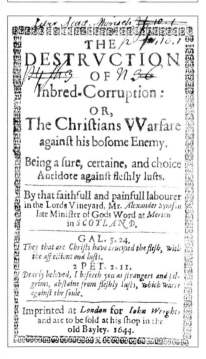

Clockwise from top left:

14 The appetite of the reading public, at all social levels, for scandalous trials was endless.

15 This detail from Marcantonio Raimondi's *Amori degli Dei* (1524) not only presents another sexual position but it combines classical allusions and bestiality.

16 This work by Alexander Symson, The *Destruction of Inbred-Corruption* (London, 1644), purports to contain the 'choice antidote against fleshly lusts'.

LES
FVNERAILLES
DE SODOME ET DE SES
FILLES, DESCRIPTES EN
vingt Sermons fur l'Hiftoire de
Moyfe en Genefe, cha-
pitre 18. & 19.

PLVS VN AVTRE SERMON,
fur le Pfeaume 34.dont l'occafion fera
deduicte en fon lieu.

Le tout par R. LE MAÇON dict DE LA
FONTAINE, Miniftre de l'Euangile
en l'Eglife de la langue Fran-
çoife en Londres.

Reueu & corrigé de nouueau en cefte derniere impreßion.

Liure grandement vtile & neceffaire pour ap-
prendre à bien & fainctement viure.

Matth.3. verf.2.
Amendez vous : car le Royaume des cieux eft prochain.

À LONDRES,
Par RICHARD FIELD, demeurant aux
Black-Frieres. M. DC. X.

This page, from top:

17 Robert le Maçon's *Les Funerailles
de Sodome* (London, 1610) was but
one of many works stressing the link
between the destruction of Sodom
in the Bible and the toleration of
'unnatural' vices by a society.

18 This detail from Albrecht Dürer's
The Men's Bath (*c.*1497) was almost
certainly meant to be amusing and
full of innuendo.

Facing page, clockwise from top left:

19 The eroticism of Renaissance
classicism and its fascination with the
adolescent male form is readily
apparent in this detail from Albrecht
Dürer's (?) *Martydom of St Sebastian*
(*c.*1500).

20 Yet again, Mirabeau's *Ma
Conversion* (Berlin, 1798) attempted
to shock and subvert social
conventions.

21 The amusing eroticism of the
dagger and the mule's arse is obvious
and attests to the easy sensuality of
late Renaissance sensibilities.

22 Leonardo da Vinci's *Measurements of the Human Body* clearly elevates the male form to its apotheosis.

23 In this charcoal copy of Rembrandt's *Rape of Ganymede* one sees the complete transformation of the myth from the seduction of an adolescent male to the less sexually threatening abduction of a child.

24 This detail from E. Fairfax's *Discourse of Witchcraft* gives some idea of the misogynistic portrayals of women that one encounters in this period.

Matthew Hopkins Witch Finder Generall

My Imps names are

Holt

1 Ilemauzar
2 Pyewackett

Jarmara

Sacke & Sugar

3 Pecke in the Crowne
4 Griezzell Greedigutt

Newes

Vinegar Tom

25 This detail is yet another representation of the dangerous woman with her lewd, lascivious and unnatural practices.

Franc. Hotmanni I.C.
DE CASTIS INCE-
STISVE NVPTIIS
Difputatio: in qua
DE SPONSALIBVS ET
MATRIMONIO EX ÏVRE CIVILI,
Pontificio & Orientali
differitur.
*temģ de gradibus & nominibus cogna-
torum & adfinium.
OPVS POSTVMVM:
cui adiectus eft
eiufdem HOTMANNI libellus de
SPVRIIS & LEGITIMATIONE,

LVGDVNI.
Apud IO. LERTOTIVM.
CIɔ Iɔ XCIV.

26 This detail serves as a stark reminder of the fate that awaited women who were considered deviant.

27 This work was but one of many explaining the correct, and incorrect, types of marital groupings with special emphasis on degrees of relationship which counted as incestuous.

Clockwise from above:

28 Albrecht Dürer's *The Penitent* (1510) not only highlights the masochistic aspects of flagellation but also lingers rather erotically on the male form.

29 Another detail from Mirabeau's *Hic-et-Hec* (Berlin 1798) rejects conventional morality by delighting in sadomasochistic sexuality.

30 The fascination of the reading public with adultery, incest and bestiality is apparent in the very title page of this work.

Ravillac Redivivus,

BEING A

NARRATIVE

Of the late TRYAL of

M^R· JAMES MITCHEL

A

Conventicle – Preacher,

Who was Executed the 18th of *January* laft, for an attempt which he made on the Sacred Perſon of the Archbiſhop of St. *ANDREWS.*

To which is Annexed,

An Account of the TRYAL of that moſt wicked *Phariſee* Major *THOMAS WEIR*, who was Executed for Adultery, Inceſt and Beſtiality.

In which

Are many Obſervable Paſſages, eſpecially relating to the preſent Affairs of *Church* and *State.*

In a Letter from a Scottiſh *to an* Engliſh *Gentleman.*

LONDON, Printed by *Henry Hills,* 1678.

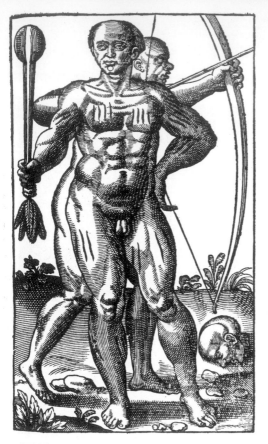

31 The natives of the New World were regularly portrayed as 'creatures of nature', as here, where there is no 'correct' shame about their nudity.

32 The barbarous, uncivilised, even demonic nature of distant lands is highlighted in this illustration.

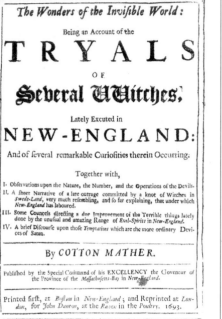

33 (*left*) There was a wide audience for works about witchcraft even at the point at which most legal authorities were advising that prosecutions should end. This account of the Salem witch-trials was one of the last and most lurid.

34 (*right*) This detail from a French book of hours (fifteenth century) not only portrays Satan as a goat (implying bestiality) but also shows a witch kissing his arse in the traditional sign of subservience to the Devil at a Sabbath.

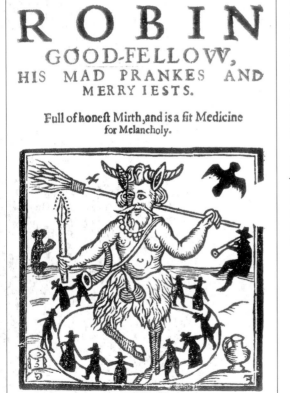

ROBIN
GOOD-FELLOW,
HIS MAD PRANKES AND MERRY IESTS.

Full of honest Mirth, and is a fit Medicine for Melancholy.

Printed at *London* by *Thomas Cotes*, and are to be fold by, *Francis Grove*, at his fhop on Snow-hill, neere the Sarazens-head. 1639

35 Imps, demons and elves in conjunction with men highlight the very real belief of most early modern peoples and societies not only in another world but in one which was inhabited by wonderful and powerful beings which could also be accessed by humans.

36 Despite the somewhat jovial modern connotations of 'Robin Good-Fellow', the sexual menace of this character is apparent in this illustration.

Since Jaquema had instigated the sex, she was judged to be fully culpable both by the lawyers and the judges. She was drowned. The court ruled that Esther was old enough to understand that she was doing wrong but the decision was taken to allow her age to be a mitigating factor. She was told that she had 'committed a detestable crime which ought not to be named' and that 'she was on track for hell and had forgotten all decency and honour and had abandoned herself to her sinful lust'. She was made to watch Jaquema being drowned and was then beaten until blood flowed from her wounds. Finally, she was banished forever on pain of being drowned if she returned. (It is not clear if the effect of this was that her entire family had to leave Geneva.) Nicolas was acquitted of any culpability because of his age. When the two girls were punished, the gathered crowd was told that Jaquema had committed a 'detestable crime that cannot be named and was possessed by the Devil'. At no point was it made officially clear to the general populace why one teenager was being drowned and another brutally beaten.

The unwillingness of early modern leaders to make the reality of lesbianism more explicitly known is most obvious in the third Genevan case from 1568. Françoise Mazel, a poor woman, was charged with molesting a fellow cleaning lady while they were sharing a bed. She eventually admitted, after torture and many depositions, that she had 'mounted' the other woman. She never gave a clear explanation for her actions but, at her execution (by drowning), she admitted she had had sex with at least three other women and two men. She also claimed she had been raped once. The city's lawyer, Colladon, gave an opinion in the case in which he stressed that 'it is such a case in which one is well advised not to publish the details of this case only that it is about a detestable and unnatural crime'. The public sentence read out at her execution followed his advice. The original phrase 'committed debauchery and fornication against nature' was replaced with 'committed a detestable and unnatural crime'. Indeed, not only did the sentence downplay her lesbianism but it went on specifically to detail her two acts of fornication with men. Anyone witnessing the execution would know that she had had sex with men and had committed some particularly evil sexual act as well but that that might be sodomy with a man or sex with an animal. In none of these cases did the Genevan government want to make explicit that women were engaging in sex with other women in the city.

However, at the upper echelons of society (especially in the later seventeenth and into the eighteenth centuries), familiarity with lesbians and their activities was relatively widespread and unremarkable. As our period progressed, men increasingly found literary references to lesbianism erotically arousing and actual lesbianism either amusing or inconceivable. This change did not go unnoticed or unopposed. The Lutheran pastor Gotthard Heidegger (1666–1711) strongly attacked novels for introducing readers, especially women, to prostitution, adultery and sexual perversion.

Moreover, this change was not overnight. In 1637, Dutch jurists had been scandalised to learn of Hendrikje Verschuur who had enlisted, disguised as a male, in the armies of Prince Frederic-Henry of Nassau and as a soldier had taken part in the siege of Breda (1637). After her disguise was exposed she was examined by Dr Nicolaas Tulp. He reported that she 'had a clitoris the size of a child's penis and the thickness of half the little finger and with that had carnal knowledge with several women, amongst others with Trijntje Barends'. The two women were 'so besotted with one another they would have liked to marry if it had been possible'. Verschuur was banished for twenty-five years after being whipped. Interestingly though, she was punished in secret and the public (as in Geneva) were 'protected' from any explicit knowledge of her activities.

The doctor's 'discovery' of an enlarged clitoris was in keeping with prevailing assumptions. It was a commonplace assumption that some women had clitorises able to function as penises. Indeed, there was a conflation of hermaphrodism (having the sexual organs of both sexes) with women having penis-like clitorises. In addition, cross-dressing was not that infrequent. In most cases, this allowed women to live and work safely in male (better-paid) trades. However, it also allowed some women to marry and in a few cases to fool their 'wives' for years – by the use of various 'implements'. In time, societies found ways to interpret these relationships as non-sexual and, thus, non-threatening. So, in the 1770s, a female transvestite living with another woman was relatively safe as long as the relationship was seen as primarily based on 'romantic sentiment' not 'sexual desire'. For example, Theodora de Verdion (d. 1802), the daughter of a Berlin architect, lived in England as a man. Her imaginative swearing and heavy drinking put paid to rumours about her true gender.

Although not a crime, it is worth passing some comment on one of the most spectacular cases of cross-dressing and living a cross-gendered life. The details of her life are fascinating: born (sometime between 1585 and 1592) Catalina de Erauso in the northern Basque town of San Sebastian she eventually entered the convent of San Sebastian the Elder along with her two elder sisters. She escaped from the convent and during three days she transformed her clothing to that of a young page-boy. In this disguise, she made her way to Peru in 1603. After twenty years, she revealed her true identity to the bishop of Guamanga (Chile) who returned her to the convent life in Peru. Investigations proved she had never taken final vows and she was released (despite stringent Spanish laws against cross-dressing) to return to Spain. At some point around 1630 she returned to the New World and this interesting personage, known, variously as La Monja Alférez or Antonio de Erauso disappeared from the historical record. An unsubstantiated report placed her death in 1650.

Her memoirs are the most intriguing aspect of her life to survive. As Michele Stepto says in the introduction to her translation (with Gabriel Stepto):

> For centuries, the Spanish-speaking world has been fascinated by the story of the Basque girl with the quick temper who ran away from her convent dressed as a man and became La Monja Alférez, the Lieutenant Nun… She traveled to the Americas in 1603, became a soldier, fought in the conquest of Chile. She enjoyed the attentions of other women, killed her brother in a duel, gambled and brawled her way through the mining towns of the Andean highlands. She killed and maimed, spent time in jail… she claimed the privilege of nobility to escape torture, and proclaimed herself a heretic to escape hanging. When finally cornered, after twenty years of masking, she revealed her secret – she was not only a woman, but an intact virgin, a piece of news, far from condemning her, brought her a brief celebrity in the Baroque world. In 1624, she returned

to Europe, where she earned from the Spanish king a military pension, and from the pope permission to continue her life in men's clothing.

She lived in a period of transition in which laws relating to women's place and behaviour were largely ineffective while, at the same time, society was increasingly finding ways to re-evaluate and re-interpret non-normative female sexualities and lifestyles in ways designed to be less troublesome to a male-dominated world.

Indeed, by the end of the century the attitude had clearly changed. In October 1691, Constantijn Huygens (the younger) in his diaries noted that Jacoba van Beuningen had begun a relationship with a Miss Splinter after having her husband confined for insanity. He commented that she had appeared in public with love bites given her by her lover and that guests to their home had seen a wax dildo lying openly about the house in various locations. This blasé attitude is in marked contrast to that seen in the earlier cases but very much in line with events in the next century, the age of the Enlightenment.

It was this period that saw the first use of the term 'lesbian'. William King wrote a satirical attack on the Duchess of Newburgh after losing a debt case to her. In *The Toast* (1736) he referred to her as a 'lesbian'. Indeed, the use of the term brings to the fore, yet again, the question of the role of categories, words and definitions in shaping reality. Many scholars would hold that the 'category' cannot exist without a widespread acceptance of the idea of a lesbian and lesbianism as a distinct 'type' of person and lifestyle. However, the term clearly pre-dates the psycho-sexual debates of the late nineteenth century (and thereafter). Also, this line of argument overlooks the existence of other early modern words for lesbians and lesbianism. For example, there are repeated references to tribades and tribadic women in addition to descriptions relating to specific sexual acts. One sees fricatrices (those who rub), subigatrices (those who work a furrow), or the more obvious clitorifantes. Thus, there were names for the individual women who engaged in same-sex acts with other women as well as their actual acts. The overall behaviour was also named: 'evil malignities', 'fouling' and 'sodomitical filthiness'.

In addition, there were discussions about the relationship of these tribades to the wider human species. How many genders were there? Some said there were three: male, female, and male sodomites. Others postulated a different three: male, female and hermaphrodites (who were most often seen as biologically female). Some placed the distinctions between male/female and effeminate males. All of which overlooked, as we have seen, attitudes to paederasty and most of which completely ignored lesbianism.

As attitudes began to change and lesbianism became more 'visible' in literature and among the social élites the number of cases increased. This should not suggest an increase in the activity but rather an alteration in society's willingness to discuss the behaviour in public. Lesbians were no longer being executed for vague 'unnatural acts' but were being lampooned in print and drooled over in erotic literature. At the same time that historians have been able to identify the development of a subculture of 'gay' males, lesbianism seems to have become more socially acceptable as it moved from being a sin that threatened a male-dominated society to an activity that amused and aroused that same masculine world.

From the very top of society in the last century of our study we see a greater openness to lesbianism. It was not being accepted or approved, rather it was being discussed with a certain censoriousness. Lesbianism was being met with gossip and giggles rather than gallows and gibbets. Thus, Queen Christiana of Sweden (1626–89) came to the throne as 'king' in 1650. She refused to marry her cousin Karl X Gustav naming him, instead, crown-prince. She almost always dressed as a man and eventually abdicated in 1654 having tired of the restraints placed upon her as a female monarch. Likewise, rumours of the lesbian or bisexual activities and proclivities of Queen Mary and Queen Anne of England were rife. In Mary's case this seems only fair as King William was widely rumoured to be more interested in adolescent males than women. Both women had multiple pregnancies which seem in no way to have quieted the court gossips.

Similar charges were laid against Marie-Antoinette. Clearly, there were political motives (not all from revolutionaries) for accusing the queen of sexual deviance. Nevertheless, there was also a widespread acceptance of the overall truthfulness of the queen's bisexuality. Thus, an English writer, Hester Thrale Piozzi, said in 1789 that: '[she is] at the Head of a Set of Monsters call'd by each other Sapphists, who [follow] her Example; and deserve to be thrown with the [male sodomites who have the same tastes] into Mount Vesuvius'. Indeed, it is a historical irony that opponents of the *ancien régime* attacked the queen for her sexual libertarianism. The revolution that deposed her subsequently de-criminalised sodomy – and then turned a few weeks later to outlaw female clubs.

However, this rather ironic end to the tale is taking us too quickly to the end of the period. The last half of the eighteenth century is rife with detailed cases involving lesbians both in court and in society more generally. It is these cases which will bring us to the very threshold of an era in which the greatest monarch of that century, Queen Victoria, could not even conceive of the activity. During the Enlightenment, lesbianism seemed to be coming into the wider public domain. Fifty years later it had become inconceivable. As we shall see, there is nothing in the cases that would suggest this amazing reversal of fortunes.

Lesbianism for most of the eighteenth century was still punishable under the law. For example, in 1750, Mooije Marijtje and Dirkje Vis were reported to the authorities by their landlady. In her testimony, she said,

> [Mooije and Dirkje] were living as if they were man and wife… feeling and touching one another under their skirts and at their bosoms… yes, she had even seen how in broad daylight while committing several brutalities Mooije lay down on Dirkje having both of them lifted their skirts and their front bodies being completely naked, [Mooije] made movements as if she were a male person having to do with a female.

The most interesting aspect of this case is the fact that the two women seemingly engaged in sexual relations in so public a manner – in broad daylight. They may have expected some repercussions but clearly they had a reasonable expectation that their relationship would not lead to their arrest.

A series of cases in Amsterdam at the time of the French Revolution (and the overthrow of the Dutch Republic by revolutionary armies) gives an excellent insight into the views of the common people, the ruling élite, and lesbians in Dutch society. However, one must constantly be aware of the rarity of lesbian trials. In the period 1730–1811, about 700 'sodomites' were prosecuted. Of these, only twelve (barely 2%) were female. Moreover, most of these cases were concentrated in 1795–98. Eleven of the twelve were tried in this period. Even with this large cache of cases lesbians never rose above 28% of 'sodomites' charged – twenty-seven men were prosecuted in addition to these women. The only other lesbian arrested was at about the same time, in 1792.

The 1792 case seems a good place to start for more than simple reasons of chronology. This was not really a case about sexuality. Rather, Bets Wiebes was arrested and charged with the murder of Catharina de Haan. She had been accused by Bartha Schuurman. To avoid arrest Bets fled into hiding dressed as a man. However, she was eventually apprehended. It became increasingly clear to the authorities that this simple murder case was extremely complex. Everything pointed to Bartha as the culprit and yet Bets continued to avoid implicating her. In the end, Bets admitted that she had been involved with both women and that, so she presumed, Bartha had killed Catharina in a fit of jealousy. (The reality may have been more complex – Bartha may have killed Catharina fearing that she would tell Bets of the burgeoning relationship between Bartha and Catharina.)

Bets confessed that she had been shielding Bartha because she believed that Bartha was actually pregnant. Pregnancy was frequently used by women on trial to avoid (or, rather, delay) torture and punishment. In the nature of the thing, it was not a long-term, sustainable defence. Once it was clear that Bartha was not, in fact, pregnant, Bets stopped protecting her. Bartha, for her part, then confessed to the crime. The court decided that she had committed the murder because of 'the envy she had entertained against Catharina [which] was situated in a strong jealousy, born from the dirty lusts that had taken place between Bets and Catharina and between Bets and herself'.

The case presents two interesting features which often appear in early modern lesbian trials. First, the actual sexual relationship was only uncovered as a consequence of another investigation. Second, the women regularly gave evidence of bisexuality rather than exclusive lesbian activities. The latter, in particular, had the result of making the male-dominated society less threatened by lesbianism. As we shall see in the case of Susanna Marrevelt (below), as long as men were able to have their needs met – and their heirs produced – they were not overly concerned about what women did with their female friends. The relative scarcity of trials arising from specific lesbian acts also highlights the secrecy of the domestic world from the ken of the male magistrates. Two men living together displaying real affection would almost certainly have raised suspicions. However, the acceptance of female romanticism, sentimentality and emotional friendship meant similar arrangements between women were not seen in the same way.

The other Dutch cases in the late 1790s simply serve to reinforce these observations. In 1796, Gesina Dekker, aged twenty-four, abandoned her husband and children. She was arrested for her sexual activities and confessed to lesbian acts with Engeltje Blauwpaard. She testified that she 'was lying on the floor with Engeltje next to her, and when they were caressing one another, Engeltje had put her finger in her womanliness, moved that finger up and down which lasted about a quarter of an hour'. There is the implication in her testimony that the genital contact had not necessarily been intended (or immediately understood) by Gesina. Rather, it had come about as the result of a tender moment that had moved into a sexual encounter.

The following year, Anna Grabou's open sensuality came to the attention of the authorities. Numerous women testified to her advances. Most had not really understood what she meant. They had then been shocked when the sexual nature of her tender advances had become apparent. However, there was more than misunderstanding involved. Most of the women chose to deal with Anna's attentions privately rather than getting her in trouble. For example, one woman testified that Anna had said to her 'I want to see you naked and if you do what I like, I shall support you. I shall give you anything your heart desires, because if I have drunk a glass of wine I am hot as fire'. The witness had not reported this conversation; it only came to light as a result of the wider investigation.

In the same year, the case of Christina Knip came to light. As with the murder case above, this started as something else – a rape case. Knip, aged forty-two, was accused of enticing a fourteen-year-old girl into her rooms, throwing her on the bed and then taking,

> a black object, looking like a big finger, from her pocket, which she tied around her body with a string. Lying across the body of the girl she put the thing with her hand into the girl's womanliness and moved it to and fro about half an hour, which caused the girl great pain.

On the surface, this appears to be no more than a cross between sexual assault and paederasty/child abuse. However, subsequent testimony made it clear that many of her neighbours knew of her sexual preferences and chose to overlook them. For example, a neighbour reported the following conversation with Knip:

> *Neighbour:* Chris, it amazes me that you don't marry.
> *Knip:* Just to fuck? If that's all I'm missing I can do [that by] myself.

It was the violence of her acts and the age of the victim that forced Knip into the spotlight of official knowledge.

A similar unwillingness to make lesbian sexual acts public is evident in the case of Susanna Marrevelt and her maid in 1798. Susanna and her husband lived in the house of his uncle. The uncle was repeatedly scandalised by Susanna's advances to the female servants. As he became aware of the relationship with the maid he became even more distressed. Eventually, he broached the subject with his nephew assuming that something would be done. Instead, he was appalled to be told: 'my wife can do as she wants. If I'm satisfied, it's nobody's business. It's none of your concern'. The uncle then threatened to drive them from his home. In the end, the scandal became so widely known that the authorities became involved.

A much more dramatic case was prosecuted the same year. Anna Schreuder and Maria Smit were the subject of local gossip. Clearly, many of their neighbours were convinced that their relationship was more than close, sentimental friendship. One day, a neighbour climbed to their attic rooms and peered at them through a peephole. Shocked by what she was seeing, she gathered other neighbours together to witness the acts – which they did in turn from 4–6 p.m. Eventually, one of the voyeurs could take no more and shouted through the spy-hole: 'Yes, you foul whores, we can see you, why don't you get up yet, [haven't] you fouled [one another] long enough?'

The women gathered their clothes and fled, chased by the growing mob. Eventually, they (and the friends to whom they had fled) had to be rescued from the crowd surrounding their refuge by constables. The case was complicated by the polit-ical support of the two (and their three female friends) for the House of Orange. The revolutionary government that had arisen in the wake of the French advance had made such sentiments a criminal offence. Thus, even here, the case was more than simply an attempt to control sexual activities. On a more prosaic note, it is one of the few cases to give evidence of lesbian oral sex rather than simply frottage or mutual masturbation.

Despite these interesting and informative cases, the reality is that late eighteenth-century society began to re-interpret female relationships. Increasingly, they were seen as romantic and sentimental attachments devoid, for the most part, of any sexual content. Thus, Rousseau's *La Nouvelle Héloïse* presents the close 'friendship' between Claire and Julie who live happily in a country cottage. They were friends though even Rousseau admitted there might be 'something more' to their relationship.

France also gives us the case of Sophie Cottin, an infertile wife who left her husband to care for the household of her good friend Julie Vénès in the 1790s. She completely inte-grated into Julie's household. However, the multilayered nature of the relationship is apparent in Sophie's comments upon the successful delivery of Julie's third child, Mathilde. Sophie confided to her diary that 'now we are the mothers of a third child'. There is nothing in the surviving evidence to suggest a sexual relationship between the two women but there is every reason to think that one of the bonds keeping Sophie in the house was a type of unrequited love.

Similar relationships are known from places other than France. For example, in Holland (the source of so many cases already discussed), we have the relationship between Betje Wolff and Aagje Deken who were a 'couple' from 1777 until their deaths in 1804. These two authors were close friends with the leading magistrate involved in the Amsterdam trials of the late 1790s just discussed above. Although an enthusiastic prosecutor of unnatural sexual acts between women, he seems to have accepted this relationship as an example of close, romantic friendship. In that, he seems to have been correct as no proof of sexual acts survives. Nevertheless, the complexity of the relationship and society's views of it are apparent in the sobriquet given to Wolff. She was known, at the time, as the Dutch Sappho!

Wales gives us the example of the so-called Ladies of Llangollen. Lady Eleanor Butler and Miss Sarah Ponsonby were extremely well-known; they went about in identical Irish riding habits and powdered wigs. There was no question but that they lived together as a couple managing the Butler estates. Again, though, there is no direct evidence that they were sexually involved. That they were romantically attached is obvious but this was not the same thing. The former – sex – was a crime; the latter – sentiment – was acceptable, even praiseworthy.

Two cases from slightly beyond our period highlight the subsuming of lesbian genital love into romantic sentimentality and female friendship. They also expose the increasing unwillingness of society to associate something so 'common' and 'base' as genital sexuality to women of standing.

Anne Lister (1791–1840) was the product of a Britain trying desperately to hold at bay the tides of revolution and revolutionary ideas including the decriminalisation of sodomy. She was a woman who successfully avoided marriage and convinced her family to allow her to manage much of the family estate. She was a paragon of conservative Anglicanism. However, she also kept amazingly explicit diaries (largely in code) which survive. She detailed every lesbian contact she had, placing special emphasis upon female orgasms – or 'kisses'. Nor was she a mere unconscious hypocrite. In fact, she often considered her own sexuality and, on one occasion, wrote that she had 'observed upon my conduct and feelings being surely natural to me inasmuch as they were not taught, nor fictitious but instinctive'.

In the course of her life she had a string of relationships, the last of which seems to have been unrequited. Her first lover was Eliza Raine, the heiress of a West Indian planter and a slave mother. Anne then became involved with Isabella Norcliffe, a scion of another wealthy landowning family. The true love of her life seems to have been Marianna Belcombe, a woman of a good yet impoverished family. Sadly, the relationship collapsed as the result of Marianna's marriage for money. Anne then went to Paris where she was involved with another expatriate, Maria Barlow, and a French lady, Madame de Rosny. For the last six years of her life, Anne returned to her estates and became involved in an intensely romantic but seemingly non-sexual relationship with Anne Walker, a neighbouring heiress.

The second case relates to a dramatic trial in Edinburgh during the 1810s. This case served as the inspiration for the book *The Children's Hour*. In 1811, Marianne Woods and Jane Pirie, proprietors of a girls' school, were accused of being sexual lovers by Jane Cumming. Jane, whose father had served in the English East India Company, was the mixed-race and illegitimate offspring of a leading Scottish family. Her grandmother, the formidable Lady Cumming-Gordon, attempted to ruin the ladies' careers. In turn, Woods and Pirie sued Lady Cumming-Gordon for slander. In the end, they won their case but their reputations were irreparably damaged.

For our purposes, the views of two of the judges are most fascinating. The jurists who thought the women guilty of the charges said very little about their reasons for accepting the accusations. In effect, they thought there was more than enough evidence. Those who sided with the schoolteachers placed great emphasis upon the untrustworthiness of Jane Cumming both as a young impressionable girl and as the product of the sensual, exotic and erotic East. They also made clear their views on the entire subject of lesbianism and, in so doing, presaged the reputed belief of Queen Victoria who would be born in the same decade as the trial. Lord Meadowbank said 'I state as the ground of my [unwillingness to believe the accusations]… the important fact, that the imputed vice had been hitherto unknown in Britain'. Similar but more complex opinions underlie the remarks of Lord Gillies: 'are we to say that every woman who has formed an early intimacy, and has slept in the same bed with another [woman] is guilty? Where [then] is the innocent woman in Scotland?'

At the end of our period, lesbianism slipped back not into a closet or obscurity. Instead, it was re-interpreted in a manner which says much about male attitudes to women. Females were driven by their bodies and emotions. It was perfectly 'natural' that they would become involved in extremely emotional and sentimental relationships – the stuff of romantic novels. Women of the lower sort might engage in sexual acts but they were as likely to be prostitutes and fornicators. However, educated and cultured women were simply incapable of the base and unnatural acts associated with lesbian genital love. As long as they kept their private acts as secret as Anne Lister and/or provided for the needs of their husbands and families, as did Susanna Marrevelt, society was willing to put an interpretative gloss on the relationships that made them culturally acceptable and unproblematic. However, any attempt to present an overt sexuality was unacceptable but then that was increasingly true of woman's place in marital relations as well. In effect woman were allowed and presumed to be romantic, sentimental and emotional beings. They were not to be sexual beings. The advice to 'lie back and think of England' encapsulates this de-sexing and de-sexualising of women.

eight

MASTURBATION, INCEST, GROUP SEX AND SADISM

W hen courts and societies from the Renaissance to the
Enlightenment spoke of 'crimes against nature' they
were normally referring to sodomy. However, even this simple
statement hides a more complex understanding. Sodomy was
usually, both legally and commonly, perceived as fourfold, as
St Thomas Aquinas had said in the Middle Ages. There was
the sodomy between men involving anal penetration. It also
allowed for a slightly wider interpretation relating to any sex
between individuals of the same sex and could, thereby,
include non-penetrative sex of men with men or women
with women. There was also the second understanding of
sodomy, bestiality. Then, there was a third category of sodomy
relating to non-procreative acts between men and women
such as oral and anal sex. Finally, there was the 'wasting of
seed' in masturbation.

Having examined two forms of sodomy in previous chapters (with bestiality to follow) it is worth taking a few

moments to consider masturbation and other sexual acts which could also be called unnatural while falling somewhat outside the normal interpretations of the crime (and sin). These included incest, group sex, sadomasochism and youthful sexual experimentation. The latter might involve penetrative as well as non-penetrative sex, it might be self-masturbation in a group or mutual masturbation as well as a host of other inventive activities which, at other times, would be considered sodomitical. As we shall see, however, courts took the view that youthful sexuality was too complex to treat in a legalistic manner.

Masturbation, for all that it was technically sodomitical, was not often the concern of the courts. Nevertheless, as will be shown, it was an issue that greatly exercised the societies and cultures under discussion. While it was non-procreative and thus sodomitical, it was not clear that this was the best way to view the act − or, more importantly, to eradicate it. We shall examine in some detail the methods used to stop the 'solitary sin'.

Incest was a much more clear-cut crime for most. The complication was that it was not always obvious what was incestuous. In some places and times, incest referred only to blood affinity. That is, individuals were not allowed to marry siblings, aunts or uncles, or cousins to a set degree of relationship (be it first, second or third). Elsewhere, incest could also include marriage or sex between individuals not related by blood but by some pre-existing marital relationship. Thus, a nephew and aunt might be prosecuted for incest when they were only related through the uncle. This inclusion of familial and marriage relationships within the rubric of incest differs from the modern-day and means the topic warrants some careful consideration to see to what extent (if any) courts differentiated between incest by blood relatives and incest by members of an extended family.

Group sex was also a problematic area. If lesbian trials were rare (and they were) then those involving group sex were almost non-existent. Indeed, the behaviour was so bizarre on so many levels as to be almost inconceivable. Despite this rarity (which seems to be actual, rather than simply related to the survival of criminal cases), the activity was not unknown. It could take many forms: a group of men with a single prostitute, a group of men and women, and single-sex groups. As we will see, group sex baffled judges to the extent that they could not quite grasp what was going on by whom and with whom. However, they were quite clear that the behaviour was a serious crime meriting severe punishment.

Likewise, the courts were not clear what to do about sado-masochistic acts which often were a part of group sexual activity. Although a regular feature of pornographic literature from the seventeenth century onwards (and dramatic productions even earlier) as well as an element in monastic and religious devotion, it was not common enough in the sexual realm for judges to have a clear idea about the behaviour. The religious injunction to mortify the flesh as well as the emphasis placed on corporal punishment in schools (especially in England) and criminal sentences meant that physical pain was often seen as having a positive corrective or deterrent role in society. The idea that someone might enjoy being beaten let alone sexually aroused by pain was both confusing and distasteful to judges as well as salacious and fascinating to the wider public following criminal cases involving sado-masochistic acts.

Before considering the more *outré* forms of sexual behaviour it seems sensible to discuss the fourth (or perhaps, better, the first) type of sodomy: masturbation. Almost by definition it is a solitary act and for most males it is their means of introduction into sex and their own nascent sexuality. However, the early modern mind was not wholly fixated on male masturbation or, indeed, solitary masturbation. Rather, the discussions of this activity were considerably more complex and frank than one might expect.

In 1601 in his *Somme des Péchés*, Jean Benedicti encapsulated the fear that societies had about masturbation: 'men will not want to marry, nor women to take husbands, when by [masturbation] they appease their lustful appetites'. As he made clear, the threat for women was no less than that for men. Or, as Pierre de Bourdeilles (1538–1640) feared, the dildo might make men superfluous. At the very end of our period, learned men were still discussing the threat posed to women by masturbation. A German pastor Karl-Gottfried Bauer (1765–1842) wrote: 'flatulence and constipation... hypochondria... venereal disease... blood poisoning... disorder in her nervous system' were caused by masturbating while reading erotic novels. His solution was that women should not read. Likewise, Carl-Friedrich Pockels (1757–1814), a philanthropist, wrote that 'sentimental people, especially women, are [masturbators]' as they are easily excited by fantasy (novels and erotic literature). Or to put it more pithily, as Jean-Jacques Rousseau (in his *Confessions*, 1782) was ever wont to do: '[these works are] dangerous books which a fine lady finds inconvenient because they can only be read with one hand'.

The place of masturbation in female sexuality was not wholly negative, though. A book, *L'Escole des Filles*, published in 1655 and widely translated thereafter, made clear that men were not necessary for the sexual fulfillment of women and discussed diverse masturbatory techniques. Various authors throughout our period also advised the use of masturbation to satisfy a woman during (or more accurately, after) sex with a man. Tomás Sanchez (1550–1610) and Alphonsus Liguori (1696–1787) both suggested foreplay and post-coital masturbation for the woman. However, they and other authors were united in stating that sex (and, thus, foreplay or anything else) purely for pleasure was unnatural and sinful, the result of 'the excesses of a lustful personality'. For, 'even in the marriage bed, moderation must be observed – for many a man has sacrificed his health, his powers, his life in the marriage bed [through too much sex]'.

The latter quotation focuses our attention on the inherent problem these societies had with masturbation. Not only was it unnatural (in the sense of non-procreative) but it was also wasteful. It did more than waste semen capable of creating a child. It also wasted the vital strength of the male. The male was frequently advised to retain semen since it was 'the most noble moisture, the strongest physical stimulus to the body'. In a world dominated by a view of the body and health based on humours (liquids) this made perfect sense. (It also underlies the continuing debate amongst athletes about the effect of sex on sporting prowess.)

Most importantly, the fluids in the body were not unique but changeable or more accurately composed of various elements in greater or lesser quantity depending on the use and location of the fluid. Semen was simply the greatest and strongest component of bodily fluid. Its misuse through masturbation could have devastating consequences. Peter Villaume, in

1787, argued that the repeated expulsion of this fluid led to the in-rushing of fluid to fill the resulting vacuum and, in time, a physical addiction to this movement of fluids. A similar view was expressed earlier in the century by Simon-André Tissot, in his *L'Onanisme, Dissertation sur les maladies produites par la masturbation* (1760). That is, masturbation was an enervating and degenerative addiction. This explains Rousseau's assertion, while discussing his masturbatory excesses, that he had become 'so effeminate but yet indomitable'.

Mention of Villaume's essay serves to highlight the stress placed on the prevention of masturbation in the Enlightenment. In the middle ages, the stress had been placed on the 'wasting of seed'. Enlightenment thinkers were much more concerned with the preservation of the physical economy of the male and his ability to control himself by rational thought rather than to be ruled, as a beast of the field, by his physical desires. Two basic models were being juxtaposed, both dependent on a humoral (liquid) understanding of physical reality. The traditional held that these humours had to be allowed to flow (as pus, blood, sweat, etc.). The newer, Enlightenment model argued for their preservation and improvement and the avoidance, at all cost, of dissipation. However, women were told increasingly 'to flow' (i.e., to be weak); women were to ooze sentiment, emotion and romance, though not sex. They were to be women of sentiment not women ruled by their wombs. Men were entirely to contain themselves; men of reason not passion. Over-indulgence and the lack of self-control were dangerous. Masturbation, for the male, led to a narcissistic self-absorption which would lead to sodomitical attraction to other men (a type of sex with oneself).

While preparing his *Universal Revision of the Entire School and Educational System* (1785–91), Joachim Heinrich Campe (1746–1818) decided on a novel approach to the articles on the prevention of masturbation. He offered a cash prize for the best articles in the influential *Berliner Monatsschrift*, the same journal which had published Kant's essay, 'What is Enlightenment?' He asked for submissions on 'how children and young people can be spared the physically and spiritually devastating vices of unchastity in general and [masturbation] in particular, or insofar as they are already infected by these vices, how they can be healed'. From the numerous entries, Campe chose three winners and a fourth place essay; all received some prize money. Villaume's article was but one.

All of this might lead one to conclude that the negative view of masturbation was universal. It was not. There was considerable debate about what was true masturbation (i.e., a type of sodomy) and what was acceptable if unpleasant. Thus, Tommaso Tamburini, in his *Theologia Moralis* (1755), argued that mutual, male masturbation was not sodomy if there was no physical attraction between the men: 'when mutual masturbation is only intended to extend one's sexual pleasure without being drawn to that person, then it is masturbation [simply, not sodomy]'. Moreover, moralists and theologians were much more concerned with the sins involved in masturbation than they were with the loss of humoral fluid. Benedicti, whom we have already met, said, 'if a person [masturbates] while fantasising about a married woman, as well as masturbation, he is guilty of adultery; if he desires a virgin, [rape]; if he fantasises about a relative, incest; a nun, sacrilege; if he fantasises about another man, then it is sodomy'. All of this had to be understood clearly by the person masturbating and, for the Catholic, explained in detail in the confessional. The object of the lust and the circumstances had to be articulated to the confessor 'because there is on top of the evil of pollution an added sin of desire or fantasising intercourse with these persons', as the *Salmanticenses* (a circle of Carmelite theologians in Salamanca, 1631–1712) explained.

The fact that masturbation was not understood solely as a solitary activity further complicated the situation as Tamburini implied. Others might be involved and, as a result, the sin of masturbation might be compounded. This problem, much to our surprise, was seen as arising from an early age. Wet-nurses, and even mothers, were seen as threats in that they were accused of arousing the infants to soothe them into sleep. The erotic threat posed to children was only increased by the equation of the breast (in particular, the nipple) with the penis. The sixteenth century discovery of the clitoris had not altered this perception and, for example, female masturbation remained heavily focused on the manipulation of the nipples. Nipples became erect by being engorged with blood (as did the penis). Moreover, disease, especially moral and sexual depravity, could be passed from nurse to child through the nipple just as venereal disease could be transmitted by the male member. Thus, on many levels, the use of nurses (often themselves unmarried mothers) was attacked during the Enlightenment. It transmitted degenerate morals, it led to a fixation on masturbation, and it evidenced a lack of proper maternal instinct. The epitome of this degeneracy was the length mothers resorted to in an effort to rid themselves of the milk they were denying their children. Konrad-Freidrich Uden denounced mothers who preferred to give suck to puppies rather than their children or, worse (as he said of some Genevan women) who suckled other women.

The dangers, then, that beset the growing child were more than simply the accidental discovery of masturbation. The behaviour could be inculcated at an early age and lead to a debilitating and destructive addiction that would lead to weakness, at its best, and sodomy, at its worst. The fact that masturbation was hardly a private activity in an age when most people shared rooms if not beds simply made the situation worse. Indeed, boys were usually introduced to the practice rather than happening upon it by accident. Friends, schoolmates, teachers, even fathers might show a youngster what to do either intentionally or simply through being overseen due to lack of privacy. In addition, boys and young men often masturbated as couples or in groups with roommates and friends whether as students or apprentices.

The communal nature of an activity now seen as almost wholly private obviously made the socio-cultural response different from that of today. For example, jurists and theologians were concerned to differentiate between the simple act of sexual release (which might be done individually or with others) from sexual acts involving mutual attraction. The former was a sin and crime (masturbation), the latter was sodomy. However, in the adolescent the situation was even more complex. We have already seen Calvin's explanation about 'psycho-sexual' development in the discussion of paederasty above. Assigning responsibility and guilt was fraught with danger and required a case-by-case approach to the subject. Since Calvin articulated so clear an analysis of the problem of adolescent development and sexual awakening it is perhaps appropriate that a number of cases be taken not only from Geneva but largely from the period of Calvinism's development (its adolescence, as it were) under Calvin and Beza. Rather than repeating much of the discussion about paederasty, the emphasis in these cases will be on sexual acts wholly between adolescents. In effect, these cases made Geneva's leaders confront a situation where no adult was culpable and yet, crimes and sins were being committed. How they dealt with these shows both their confusion and their subtlety.

In January 1564 (the year of Calvin's death), three boys were arrested for buggery. Simon Chastel and Mathieu Convenir were both the sons of immigrants to the city. Pierre Roquet's father, on the other hand, was a citizen. Pierre (aged eight) readily confessed that he and Mathieu had tried to penetrate each other and had manipulated each other and engaged in frottage. Mathieu (aged seven) confirmed the testimony and added that their acts had made them 'sore'. Simon (aged nine), for his part, confessed that he had introduced the other boys to the behaviour. He said that he had learned how to do this from an older boy, a 'student' named Ozias Lamotte, who had molested him.

Four days before their arrest, this same Lamotte had been drowned for raping Jehan Cherubim, a boy he was tutoring to help pay for his own education. Young Jehan had told his parents about the rape over the dinner table one evening. He said that he had angered his tutor and been told to drop his breeches and bend over to be beaten. Obviously aroused by the caning as he administered it, Lamotte then raped the boy. Jehan's father was, as one might imagine, furious – all the more so since he had specifically forbidden Lamotte from beating his child fearing that it might lead to worse (on flogging and sadomasochism see below).

What is striking about these interconnected cases is the response of the court. Lamotte was drowned. Nothing at all was done to Jehan beyond his being forced to stand before the court and accuse Lamotte to his face, which he seemed to do with equanimity. However, the trio of boys (Simon, Pierre and Mathieu) were ordered to be beaten by their parents in front of a roaring fire. They were then told to cast some sticks on the fire and told that that is what would happen to them if they ever repeated the crime. In effect, they were forced to burn themselves in effigy. More intriguingly, the court then ordered the parents to ensure that the children did not see each other again. Clearly the courts feared that the temptation to repeat the sin might be too great if the children were able to consort with one another. Jehan was seen as wholly 'innocent', a victim of rape. Lamotte was wholly guilty as a rapist and child molester. The other three boys were innocent but deemed to need a strong lesson to ensure they would not re-offend or, presumably, introduce anyone else to the behaviour.

Two years later in 1566, the city's judges were presented with an even more complex case. Three students at Geneva's Academy, the training ground for Calvinist ministers, were arrested on suspicion of sodomy. All three were aged fifteen; two were from Gascony and one from Piedmont. The Italian was Bartholomy Tecia while one of the Frenchmen was named Emery Garnier and the other Théodore-Agrippa d'Aubigné. The importance of this case is heightened by the involvement of d'Aubigné who grew up to be a leading Huguenot theologian, historian and apologist. As the case evolved it became clear that the two Frenchmen, and other students, had been subjected to repeated advances by Tecia. He had made salacious comments, had wrestled nude with some of the boys and had physically molested d'Aubigné in bed one night (this later paragon of Calvinist virtues had rebuked Tecia in Latin – evidence of his learning and, perhaps, a slight language barrier).

Tecia admitted that he had been molested as a child by a doctor in Avignon. He also confessed that he had wanted to have sex with d'Aubigné and had tried repeatedly to seduce other students. In addition to being shocked by these goings-on the judges were appalled to realise that the students had discussed this amongst themselves for months before deciding to bring it to the attention of the authorities. This laxity in reporting the behaviour probably explains why the court initially arrested Tecia and his two roommates. In the end the court believed that d'Aubigné and Garnier were innocent victims who had been a bit slow in complaining. However, they also decreed that Tecia, 'because he had, from a young age, abandoned himself to committing the horrible and detestable crime of sodomy' and had tried to seduce others should be drowned. His guilt was compounded by his education by which he, better than most of his age, realised the true horror of his crime. (Even he had confessed that he knew that sodomy was the reason God had destroyed Sodom and Gomorrah.) Here age, previous sexual behaviour, sexual predation and educational status played a part in determining that a fifteen year old should be executed. Indeed, his learning produced an awareness which seems to have been the deciding factor leading to his conviction and execution.

However, Tecia's execution is the exception which proves the rule (his exceptionalism further highlights the impact of his education on the judges). In 1672, two other boys were arrested. Jacques Descles (aged eleven or twelve) and Pierre Caillati (aged nine or ten) confessed to mutual masturbation and attempted anal intercourse. Jacques admitted that he had partially penetrated Pierre but had stopped when Pierre said he was being hurt. They had also indulged in frottage. The court admonished them and ordered their parents to beat them but nothing more. Indeed, the judges were mostly interested in who had taught the boys this behaviour. There is a striking assumption that no one would come up with such ideas on their own which says something about the judges' understanding of the innocence and naïveté of the young. They said an older youth had showed them what to do though they did not know his name. The boys also said their motivation (another issue dominating the court) was 'only curiosity'.

Half a century later, André Bron (a citizen's son aged eleven) and Jean Chaix (the bastard son of a poor Genevan native) gave the same explanation for their indulgence in 'disgusting acts'. They shared a bed with a four year old, Samuel Moyne, in the house where they were apprenticed. They confessed to mutual masturbation, frottage and intercrural sex but without ejaculation or penetration. Jean said he had seen two other (perhaps older) boys, André Bernard and Paul Thibaut, doing the same. Both Jean and André admitted that Samuel had been awake and slightly involved in some of the sex as he slept in between them. They also said they had fooled around with their master's four-year-old daughter. In no case had penetration taken place. The court sentenced them to be beaten at the city's general hospital in front of the orphans and schoolchildren.

If there is one thing these cases highlight it is the extent to which the young were not only sexually active but active in groups. The cases involved more than two children with multiple 'partners'. They also concerned the courts in that it was obvious that the young were not informing adults of the sexual behaviour going on in their midst. This is in marked contrast to the apparent willingness to report adult abuse. However, it was not only other children who would keep silent as this final case will show. Nor was Tecia's age (being the oldest of the youths discussed thus far) the real issue in his execution as one might have supposed to this point.

In November 1600 two youths were arrested. Pierre du Four was the nineteen-year-old son of a leading Genevan merchant and landowner. The other youth was a cowherd named Pierre Brilat (aged sixteen) from Burdigny where the du Fours had substantial holdings – and influence. As the trial progressed it became clear that the two had been involved with one another for a few months. However, the relationship was not one of equals. Du Four regularly gave 'gifts' (i.e., payments of food and money) to Brilat after sex. Their relationship foundered when du Four attempted to limit Brilat's access to pasturage (another 'gift' previously given). Their shouting match in the meadows had turned into a fist-fight. Brilat had run home in tears and kept calling du Four a 'bugger'. The women who tended his wounds tried to silence him but it was too late; the local minister had heard his remarks.

One might think that a stray remark was unlikely to start a major investigation. However, evidence from du Four's father and the minister make it clear that they had suspected something but had been unable to get any information from the local villagers. The testimony of these same villagers is so guarded as strongly to imply that they knew about the relationship but had kept silent to protect the superior's son, a local youth and the pasturage arrangements that had developed.

Brilat broke under interrogation and confessed to repeated mutual masturbation and, eventually, anal penetration with ejaculation (the classical legal definition of sodomy). Du Four admitted to 'wrestling' with Brilat but said his mother was present. Also, as proof of his innocence, he asserted that he had fornicated with a woman – as his father well knew – and therefore was unlikely to have had sex with another male. The court was not convinced and du Four was tortured and then admitted to sex with Brilat as well as a number of other youths (singly and in groups). He continued to stress that he had never been the passive partner. Both admitted that they were well aware that they had committed a capital offence and were subsequently drowned – du Four's appeal as a citizen to the Council of Two Hundred failed to save him. As with the Tecia trial, the judges placed stress not on the participants' age (which seemed incidental) but on their awareness of their sin and the repetition of the behaviour.

If nothing else, these cases highlight how much more public sex was in the early modern period than today. Children and adolescents, even those not sexually active themselves, were usually witnesses to sexual acts by older adolescents, adults and (often) their parents. Also, sex often involved more than two people at a time though not necessarily in a group. That is two couples might have sex in the same room, if not the same bed. The public aspect of sex as well as the apparent unwillingness of people to attract the attention of authorities may partially explain the absence of cases of 'group sex'.

However, group sex in the sense of orgies was not unknown. Three cases will have to suffice to give some idea of the inventiveness of early modern adults as well as the point at which public sex involving others stopped being 'normal' and became an unnatural crime.

The first case requires us to return to the fictional world of Nicolas Chorier's *Satyra Sotadica* (1660, published in English as *A dialogue between a married lady and a maid*), and Tullia, an older married woman, and Ottavia, her younger, single friend. Here for the titillation and delight of the reader, orgies were displayed. In every case, the women initially resisted the advances of the men. They lamented their shame and horror at the prospect of an orgy. However, they eventually stopped protesting and began to enjoy what had begun as a rape. Throwing themselves into the spirit of the orgy, the reader is regaled with the details of their repeated orgasms. In this fictional world of the seventeenth century orgies were a source of arousal and amusement. In practice, courts were considerably less indulgent or amused.

In 1569, Claude Crestien and Jacques Molliez were arrested by Geneva's authorities for indecency and being 'libertines'. They had been arrested because of the pregnancy of Pernette Chappuis, a chambermaid. She had told how she had had sex with Crestien as well as two brothers (Bernard and Jacques Molliez) and the son of a local nobleman, Lord Veygier, and Pierre de Vaux (the valet of another local worthy, Lord D'Avullier). The court was appalled to learn that each man had had sex in turn while the other four remained in the room. They were fascinated by a number of aspects of the case: in what order had the men had sex; where, exactly, were the other four; what had they been doing.

Apparently, the order was based on social precedence with Veygier's son having sex first followed by de Vaux, the gentleman's valet. They had agreed by mutual consent on the order – the fact that this had been discussed truly shocked the court. The person who was next had sat on the foot of the bed awaiting his turn while the other three stood in the room. Both men who were being questioned stressed that at no time had the three men awaiting their turn actually touched one another or themselves. That is, there was no genital contact between the men nor were they engaging in group masturbation and voyeurism. They were – or so they claimed – patiently waiting their turns. Crestien and Molliez (the only two who had failed to avoid arrest) were flogged in public and perpetually banished on pain of death should they return.

If this case upset the authorities, their successors two decades later (a scant ten years before the publication of Chorier's erotic tales of lesbianism and orgiastic sex) were even less impressed with the case of six men arrested for group sex. Even more bizarre, the case was truly international and ecumenical. One of the men, Girardin Dupuis, was local (and aged about fifty). A youth, Estienne Chappuis (aged fifteen) was a citizen's son who had travelled widely in Germany, Switzerland and Italy. Jean Chaffrey, a soldier from France (aged twenty) was also arrested. The other three men were slaves on Bernese galleys on Lake Geneva: Tartare bin Mohamet, Ali Arnaud, and Hassan (also a Turk). They were former Muslims who had been captured by the Venetians, converted to Catholicism then sold on to the Savoyards for use on Lake Geneva where they had fallen into Bernese hands and been converted to Protestantism.

The sexual antics, and histories, of the men deeply troubled the judges. The immediate details of the orgy were amazing enough. All six men had been eating and drinking in a local inn, La Cloche. They had been stroking and kissing one another (as well as other youths in the inn). Money, food and drink were flowing rather freely. Because of the late hour, Dupuis and Chaffrey (both soldiers) decided to spend the night. They got into a bed where they were joined by Hassan and Ali. Chaffery said that Dupuis 'the Christian' had had sex with one of the 'galley slaves' at least twice that night. He had had sex three times; he had been a virgin up to that point. The first time he had engaged in frottage and ejaculated into his shirt. He had then penetrated the Turk twice.

The teenager Chappuis admitted he had allowed himself to be penetrated by Tartare (because he had the smallest penis). Tartare had solicited him by saying that he preferred sex with males to women because 'women were too "big" and that it was the custom of the galleys'. He had then had sex but, at the Turk's request, had been on top, astride the Turk. Tartare confirmed the details but said the youth had initiated the sex. He also admitted, when asked, that such behaviour was illegal in his homeland (Turkey) and resulted in enslavement in the galleys.

Having satisfied themselves with the basic details of the orgy, the judges then sought information on the past behaviour of the defendants. Chappuis said he had been employed by a German merchant as a servant and had travelled to Fribourg and Basel where he had taken service with an Italian (at the young age of eleven). In Milan, a 'gentleman' had given him some food and drink; he was then thrown on a bed and almost raped. His cries had resulted in his being struck so hard he was sick but the assault had stopped. Later he had had sex with another gentleman in Rome and been fondled by a cardinal.

Dupuis had no less a chequered history. He had been in galley service for eighteen years as a result of his involvement in a murder. He had had sex in the galleys (for example with a Greek named Paraclites) and, for two years, had been involved with a youth (aged about nineteen) from Piedmont. He strongly denied, though, that he had ever been prosecuted for sex with a mare. Chaffrey, as we have seen, was a virgin until that night. The Turks gave fewer details but made it clear that sex was fairly common amongst the galley slaves and that the more handsome youths were passed around when they first entered 'service' in the galleys.

Chaffrey's single night of orgiastic passion ended as it did for the others. They were all executed though there is some implication in the dossier that Dupuis may have been released and banished. If this is the case it might be that his 'owners' had intervened to save the life of a trained galley slave who was already sentenced to a life in chains. In any case, the reaction of the judges in practice shows the extent to which a simple reliance on literature is dangerous. On stage and in novels, the literature of the time might suggest a mildly amused attitude to a whole range of 'deviant' behaviour: for example, cross-dressing, orgies, lesbianism and paederasty. However, the few cases above make it clear that what might amuse a metropolitan, educated, sophisticated audience and what was socially tolerated in reality were two very different things. The truth was simple: almost anyone putting into practice these types of behaviour risked a painful execution.

What is noticeable by its absence in most of these trials is anything sexually adventurous. True, the quantity of partners as well as their genders is interesting but, except for the case of Tartate and the young Estienne, sex was fairly 'normal'. Even sex between men seems to have been confined to mutual masturbation, frottage and anal penetration. There is little or no mention of oral sex, complex positions or, most interestingly, any fetishism. As we have seen in the chapter on sodomy, oral sex was not unknown and the shaving of a woman's privates is known from at least one case already discussed. Needless to say, these remarks serve as an introduction to a brief discussion of some more surprising sexual activities – in this case, sadomasochism.

As the behaviour is extremely rare, one case will have to suffice. However, even this case highlights the conventional nature of sex in the early modern period. In 1707, Samuel Self, among others, was prosecuted in Norwich for 'gross and unnatural' behaviour. He had come to the attention of the authorities when he filed for divorce without alimony against his wife on a charge of adultery with their male lodger, John Atmeare. Clearly, he had assumed that his wife would go quietly. In fact, she exposed a very complex household. Samuel, a bookseller whose business had fallen on hard times, had sublet various parts of the family home to several lodgers: Mr Atmeare, Mr and Mrs Morris (Robert and Jane) as well as a guest (the young spinster, Sarah Wells) and a maid-of-all-work, Susan Warwick.

It appears that Samuel had tried to encourage Atmeare and his wife into intimacy in a Machievallian attempt to catch her in adultery and rid himself of his spendthrift wife. In actuality, they had also engaged in a number of sexual exploits involving the caning and birching of one another. For the most part, Robert Morris seems to have remained aloof (though not ignorant) of the proceedings. His wife was frequently beaten by the other men and women. They also were beaten in turn by each other. On any number of occasions, the women were exposed for the viewing of the others and various guests. Also, there had been multiple couplings in shared beds. However, and here the conventionality is obvious, sex seems always to have been between men and women in the missionary position regardless of how many couples were having sex or how many bystanders were watching or how many beatings had preceded the sex. Although the men beat one another they did not engage in any sexual contact. Nor, it seems, did the women. Except for the number of people in the room either watching or having sex and the birchings, this is hardly interesting at all.

In other words, even where sadomasochism (that is, birching) was a part of sex, the inventiveness of the participants was clearly limited and very much in keeping with the views expressed by Daniel Defoe in his treatise on *The Uses and Abuses of the Marriage Bed* (in which everything other than the missionary position was an abuse). Indeed, it is likely that they were acting out fantasies they had encountered in pornographic and erotic texts passing (legally and illegally) through Self's bookstore. Later, though, there are a number of examples of works specialising in this sort of sexual activity. In 1718, an English translation of *A Treatise on the Use of Flogging in Veneral Affairs* appeared. Later, in 1749, James Cleland had devoted an entire chapter of *Fanny Hill* to flagellation – though the work was prosecuted for its sodomitical elements.

Flagellation had a long and somewhat distinguished history. It was very much a part of religious life as a way of mortifying the flesh especially in medieval Catholicism (later, Counter-Reformation Catholicism found the practice slightly more disturbing). It became uniquely associated with the English as the 'English Vice' perhaps because of its prevalent use in schools. Also, it was so much a part of illicit sexual activity in England, that William Hogarth included a bundle of birch branches in his *A Harlot's Progress* (1730). As we have seen in the case of Lamotte (above), Continentals often took a different view of the beating of children. Indeed, many early modern French and Italian schools forbade teachers – in their contracts – from thrashing students fearing it might to lead to worse behaviour.

Amongst Continentals in general and Catholics in particular there was an extensive history of discussion and debate about the use of flagellation and its possible relation to psycho-sexual problems. In 1600, the German doctor John Meibom tried to offer a pre-psychoanalytical explanation for people who were 'stimulated to venery [sexual arousal] by strokes of rods and worked up into a flame of lust by blows'. Earlier, the practice had gained notoriety because of the excesses of a prominent confessor and religious leader in the Netherlands, Cornelius Adriasen. He led a group of maidens and matrons whom he regularly beat as part of their penance. However, he also 'used gently to rub their bare thighs and posteriors with willow and birch rods'. This case became famous by its inclusion in Meteren's *Latin History of the Netherlands* (1568) so much so that a priest beating a female penitent became known as the 'Cornelian Discipline'.

Eventually, the problems associated with flagellation (as religious penance) and sexual arousal (sadomasochism) led to an open debate by Catholic theologians. Abbé Boileau in his *The History of Flagellants and the Correct and Perverse Use of Rods among Christians* (1700) attacked the practice while Thiers' *Critique of the 'History of the Flagellants'* not only defended the practice but attacked Boileau for giving ammunition to Protestant opponents of Catholicism. In reality, as the previous chapters have shown, flagellation was about as bizarre as early modern sexual practice became. Sex was, by its very nature, too quick, too public and (often) too dangerous to develop into more innovative forms and fetishes. At its most 'deviant', sex from the Renaissance to the Enlightenment remained relatively conventional.

Although quite distinct in some ways, incest has its place in the foregoing discussion. Given the public nature of sex, especially by family members and adolescents, it is perhaps surprising that incest is as uncommon as it appears to have been. Nevertheless as a few cases will show it was not unknown. Nor, because of the inclusion of incest 'by marriage' was it entirely what one might expect. Indeed, as we shall see, the 'appearance' of incest was also a concern. A few cases during the height of Calvin's influence in Geneva, a period noted for an emphasis on moral purity and a focus on familial stability, throw an interesting light on the differences between the theories of judges and ministers and the reality within their societies.

Claude Bontemps was arrested in 1546 for incest and adultery with his sister and trying to poison his wife. The details of the case are straightforward and uninteresting. He confessed to the adulterous relationship and had come to the attention of the authorities when he tried to buy arsenic from a number of apothecaries for no apparently good reason. What is interesting in the case, though, is the charge of incest. His sister, Maurise, was in fact his sister-in-law and not a blood relative. Moreover, the public sentence at his execution was as opaque as any pronouncement for lesbianism. He was being condemned for 'execrable crimes warranting grave corporal punishment'.

A decade later Thivent Taccon, Christobla Sertoux (his wife's niece) and Pierre Dentant were prosecuted for incest, bribery and perjury. Again, the case was fairly simple. Thivent had had an affair with Christobla and she had become pregnant. To cover up the pregnancy and, it appears, to allow the relationship to continue, Thivent arranged for his servant Pierre to marry his niece and present the child as his own. The conspiracy began to unravel when the pregnancy became obvious and Pierre proved less than willing to accept the punishment for fornication (anticipating the marriage) let alone to allow the affair to continue. All three were banished for ten years and Thivent was ordered to pay to the orphans in the city's general hospital the sum he had intended to use to bribe his servant. Despite the state's earlier reticence the public pronouncement in this case made the crime clear: they were guilty of 'incest and cohabitation in fornication despite the express prohibitions of the Word of God'.

An identical case in 1564 saw Jacques Rivit, a naturalised citizen, beheaded and buried under the gibbet for adultery with the sister of his first wife (while married to his second wife, Gonine Sengard) and trying to get a servant to marry her to hide her pregnancy and to allow the relationship to continue. The servant, Corajod, got cold feet for exactly the same reasons as Pierre Dentant above. Despite his qualms he agreed to continue with the plan in return for even more money. A family friend, Jean Losserand (whom we have already met), was also prosecuted (and placed in the stocks for two hours) for knowing about the relationship but saying nothing – indeed, he had perjured himself in the original trial.

Two brief cases (one from 1557 and the other much later in 1627, for the sake of comparison) highlight the problems that might arise from even the appearance of impropriety. These also make clear the Calvinist method of trying to avoid actual sin and crime by stopping any behaviour that might result in illegal or immoral activity. In the earlier case, André Plot (a Catholic) and his infirm aunt, Jehanne Conot, were arrested for sharing a bed despite his mature age which had caused 'a great scandal amongst all his neighbours and because this [behaviour] is not decent, commendable nor honest' and should not be repeated 'to avoid all suspicion and scandal'.

In the later case, Jean du Perril (a citizen, aged twenty-seven) was prosecuted along with his mother, Claudine Jonsier (aged fifty-eight) for sharing a bed in an inn while on a business trip to Chambéry. His wife Jeanne Pela (aged thirty-three) had complained that not only did they frequently share a bed but had actually de-loused each another wearing nothing more than their shirts. Both the defendants maintained that they had done nothing wrong or untoward or, more interestingly, uncommon. They had shared a bed on the trip because of 'their poverty'. Jean often got in his mother's bed because she was 'possessed by some malign spirits [mentally troubled]' and his presence comforted her; also, he and his wife were not on good terms. The court was much less lenient and banished both of them on pain of death should they have the temerity to return.

Clearly, as most of these cases stress, incest rarely involved blood relatives. Also, the courts were very concerned about adults sleeping together who were not either of the same sex or married to one another. Any other arrangement might lead to illegal sexual behaviour and would certainly produce a scandal. One final case (which has already been discussed) from 1595 presents a truly complex mix of lesbianism, incest and child abuse and seems a fitting way to bring this section of the volume to a close.

It will be necessary briefly to recap the case. Jacquema Gonet, a teenage serving girl, was drowned for corrupting the morals of her master's two children: Esther and Nicolas Bodineau, aged fifteen and nine respectively. Jacquema and Esther had molested one another while in bed. Jacquema had initiated the sex and admitted she had had sex with others and had seen other adolescents having sex in her home village. She had also told Esther that even young boys were able to get erections, 'make their members longer', as she had seen some of the village boys do. They had then molested Nicolas and he had mentioned something to his mother but she had not taken him seriously. The courts were especially concerned by the mother's apparent lack of interest and she was arrested and investigated for a brief while as part of the wider case. The court decided that Jacquema, herself clearly a teenager (though her exact age is not noted), was drowned for – according to the public sentence – 'having committed a detestable crime that ought not to be named and for being possessed by the Devil'. Esther was flogged and banished forever on pain of death for her part in the sex. The lawyers advised that only her age and her passivity in initiating the activities should result in her life being spared. Nicolas was deemed to have been wholly innocent, a victim of incest and 'rape' (child abuse).

This case rather neatly closes this chapter. A court is seen struggling with issues of age and accountability. Initiative and passivity are seen as mitigating elements. There is great concern about what should and should not be said in public about 'deviant' sexual activities. It also highlights the ready access even the youngest members of early modern societies had to sexual activity. All they had to do was look around or listen. Sex was everywhere in a world of over-crowded rooms and shared beds. Finally, despite the best efforts of magistrates, lawyers and theologians sex and talking about sex were very much a part of life. This world, for all it punished sexual acts it deemed unnatural and deviant, was not coy.

nine

ANIMALS, 'MONSTERS' AND DEMONS

In addition to the various permutations of couplings already discussed, the societies from the Renaissance to the Enlightenment recognised a number of other unnatural sexual acts. The most common, one would suppose, was bestiality. However, little evidence survives about this type of sex because it was something normally done in the rural countryside, and sadly, most of the extant records come from urban communities. Later in our period, some societies (especially England) began to consider some types of people as 'monstrous' or non-human. Eunuchs, especially *castrati*, were frequently deemed to be a third category of being, neither male nor female and – more importantly – not quite human. Earlier in our period, a similar fascination surrounded hermaphrodism. Finally, all societies considered sex with demons and Satan not only possible but frighteningly common as an essential part of witchcraft. This final chapter, then, will consider these types of sexual relations which were unnatural in their own way.

It needs little comment to explain why sex with animals was considered unnatural. Also, it takes less imagination to understand that this type of sexual contact was probably relatively common in rural communities especially amongst animal herders who spent lots of time alone with their animals. In most urban areas, the relative lack of availability of larger animals – and of privacy – made this activity less common. Nevertheless, one must never underestimate human ingenuity or the strength of the (male) sex drive. Geneva's copious criminal records do contain a few cases of bestiality. Although a highly urbanised state, Geneva was also small enough (10,000–20,000 in our period) for many people to have gardens and pastures within easy reach of the city. Thus, there was sufficient opportunity for bestiality to take place and enough potential urban witnesses to ensure that some cases made it to trial and, hence, survive to this day.

In 1678, Jean-Marc Tournier (aged eighteen), a cowherd from Burdigny, was arrested on suspicion of having had sex with cows. The number of witnesses involved in the case is amazing for a rural event. The first, Jean Pitet (aged forty-five), said he had been passing by a field when he had seen a youth having sex with a cow. He had shouted out, 'Hey, bugger, I can see you're doing something foul with that cow'. However, he was too far away to intervene or identify the culprit clearly, and could only say he was a teenager with a big grey hat. This sent the authorities scrambling to round up everyone in the local village (Burdigny), first to find anyone fitting the description and second to see if any more details could be uncovered.

The most obvious teenager seems to have been Jean-Marc. A city prosecuting magistrate went to his house to bring him (and his mother, Nicolarde Brassard) in for questioning. She said he was away from home at the moment gathering firewood. The official left a summons ordering him to appear by a set date or be fined. In addition, depositions were taken from most of the extended Tournier family and their neighbours: Jean Tournier (an official in the local administrative region of Peney, aged sixty-eight), his wife (Bernardine Joly, aged fifty) and his brother Daniel (aged sixty-six); Jean Tournier (aged fifty-five), his wife (Odette Bastard, aged fifty), and their son (Hugues, aged thirty); two other members of the Bastard family (Jacquema, aged sixty-two and Jeanne, aged forty); Gabriel Tournier (aged twenty-four); Pierre de la Rouge (aged forty-two); Pierre Bourgeois (aged forty-two); Pierre Tournier (aged forty-three); Daniel-François Lechière (aged fifty) and his wife (Pernette Rendu, aged forty); François Daquet (aged fifty); Pierre Ferroux (aged forty-two); Abel Maré (aged twenty-seven) and Henry Maré (aged sixty); David Reymond (aged thirty-eight); Pernette Foriaud (aged fifty); and Jean Revillard (Jean-Marc's cousin, aged fifteen).

The questioning of most of the village's population presented both the court and us with a complex case and an example of effective stonewalling by a tightly knit community. It was clear that Jean-Marc regularly herded the cows alone which was already suspicious. Most villages, seemingly, were encouraged to have herding done by at least two people if not more to prevent bestiality. Everyone knew the boy who was the village's chief cowherd. There were rumours that he had fornicated with a young girl who made butter but no one had heard anything about a predilection for cows (or horses). Still, there was widespread awareness that his desire to herd alone was peculiar. However, most of the villagers knew that this was in part because he had argued with his brothers who did not want to herd the cows. It seems he had decided it was easier to do the work himself than to argue with them every day.

When Jean-Marc finally presented himself the court could not get to the bottom of the case. No one who regularly herded fit the description which had been given. He explained that 'he liked to be alone and his brothers wouldn't let him think and annoyed him'. The initial witness, Jean Pitet, was brought in and said Jean-Marc was not the person he had seen as his hair and hat colour were wrong. As the case continued, other rumours began to spread. Jean Revillard was said to have refused ever to herd with his cousin again because Jean-Marc had molested a cow once while he was there. There was also the implication that Jean-Marc's brothers had been threatening the other villagers to keep them quiet. The court was convinced that Jean-Marc's explanation that 'he liked to think' (in peace and quiet) was not credible – and that he had simply got a new hat. The judges were also positive that pressure was being brought to bear on Jean Revillard and that his family had been told they would be burned out of their house if the boy said anything against Jean-Marc. Despite all of these concerns, the silence coming from Burdigny was complete and the case eventually collapsed.

This case gives us some fascinating insights into the prosecution of early modern justice. On the basis of a single report, an entire village was hauled in for questioning. Also, there is a clear assumption that 'clothes make the man' or, at least, that villagers have only one set of outer clothing and can be easily identified (at a distance) as a result. The inability of the court to break family solidarity is interesting as well. These villagers – as in other cases we have seen – were united in denying knowledge of any wrong-doing and in protecting one of their own. Both the court and the locals identified the young teenager, Jean Revillard, as the chink in the villagers' armour. If Jean could be broken, the truth might come out. The ability of Jean-Marc's brothers to silence Jean and their apparent willingness to use extreme violence to that end is revealing. In the end, local and familial solidarity was greater than state pressure. More importantly, a local community seems to have been willing to tolerate bestiality rather than see a well-liked (and useful) local lad burnt at the stake.

A case eighteen years before, in 1660, had proven almost as complex. Pyramus Mermilliod (aged sixteen or seventeen) who was a servant of the syndic, Esaia Colladon (of the prestigious family which had given Geneva numerous ministers and legal advisors) was arrested for molesting a cow. The chief witness against the youth was Danielle Livron (aged thirty), another of Colladon's servants. After dinner, the syndic had asked for some water and she had dashed to the stable to fetch some. There she had seen 'Pyramus, the cowherd, directly behind a red cow, holding his manly member outside [his trousers] in his hands against the [genitals] of the cow as she had seen to her great horror'. She had run back to the house but no one was there. She had only been able to find the shepherdess (Catherine Labouz, aged twelve or thirteen) who confirmed that Danielle had told her the tale and that Danielle had been clearly distressed.

One of the city's prosecuting magistrates then went to the stable to examine the 'crime scene'. He returned and reported that he had measured both the height of the cow's 'fundament' and Mermilliod's 'privates'. His conclusion was that 'the former was one French royal foot higher than the latter and the act, therefore, unlikely'. In addition, Mermilliod, when questioned, presented the court with a baffling explanation for his action. He said, 'it was true that he held one of his hands against the cow and had held his manly member with his other hand but only so he could urinate on the cow's fundament to kill the fleas having been told at Jussy that this was a good remedy'. Solomon, a cowherd now working in Vaud, had taught him this cure. He denied having any desire for sex with the cow and apologised for any scandal he might have caused. He said 'he couldn't think of any explanation' when told that the shepherdess had testified that he had used the word 'bugger' when trying to explain his actions. When asked if he knew of any buggers he said (*à la* the bogey monster), 'yes, but he was in the mountains'. Since the urban magistrates had no way of knowing if he was telling the truth and there was only one witness, who might easily have panicked having misunderstood what she was seeing (depending on the angle of her vision) they left Mermilliod 'to God's judgement' and released him.

A similar case, with 'forensic' evidence playing an important part, took place three years (1663) after Mermilliod's trial. André Chabrey related that he had gone to arrest François Bosson with some officers of the law as a result of the testimony of a chambermaid. He had fled when challenged. A chase had ensued along the Rhône to Bosson's lodgings where he had finally surrendered himself though he had refused to say anything. Chabrey then went off to the stable with a maid to examine the 'crime scene' and the cow in question. He reported, 'I found that the height of the said Bosson was high enough and that of the said cow was medium and that the place that is behind the said cow was slightly raised because of some quantity of dung that was there'. He concluded that this made the assault physically practical although both the maid (Estienna Duvillard, aged thirty) and her master, Noé Remilly (aged forty-five), both testified that the dung had not been there when the attack supposedly took place.

Remilly said that he had been told by Duvillard that she had seen Bosson 'standing behind a young, black cow with his one hand moving aside the cow's tail and his other hand on his flies'. She had been horrified and screamed in a loud voice, 'My God, Bosson, what are you doing there?' He had not replied at all and had later spoken to her as though nothing had happened. Remilly had never heard anything else bad about the man. Duvillard concurred, saying she had seen Bosson 'behind a black cow with his hand on the cow's [genitals] holding aside its tail with his elbow and his other hand on his flies'. She had said, 'Hey, My God, Bosson, what are you doing there?' She added that, 'he said nothing but it is true that she noticed that he jumped somewhat and immediately left the said cow'. However, he was back at work later and he was a good worker.

When he was questioned, Bosson simply denied being in the stable. He admitted that he had lied to Remilly when he had asked to leave work early to buy grain. He had gone to his brother-in-law's house in the rural village of Versoix. He said this was to have work done on his tools since it was cheaper there than in Geneva. However, he could give no explanation for his lie about the grain (he implied it was because he did not want Remilly, or anyone else, knowing his business) or why he had not spoken to his brother-in-law despite spending two nights in the village. He said it was because he was there on business and not a social call and that they had chatted briefly. He could not explain why his wife was concerned about his whereabouts (she had gone to Remilly looking for him) since he had left money and grain in plain view on the windowsill. Also, he admitted that he had been wrong to run from the officers but could not explain his flight. Taken together, the court thought there was more than enough reason to apply judicial torture. However, he continued to deny even being in the stable. In the end the case came down to his word against Duvillard's. The city released him but decided to banish him on pain of a flogging if he ever returned.

Earlier in the seventeenth century (1636) another case of bestiality had collapsed because of the lack of other witnesses. Petreman Milliau (aged seventeen) had been denounced by his master. Ami Chappuis (aged sixty) testified that he had seen 'the said Petreman... holding a horse in an embrace from behind and thrusting against it... and had continued some little time in this action'. Petreman denied the accusation and said, in reply, that he had argued with Chappuis the day before. As a result of the argument, he had left Chappuis' service and his house. Indeed, Chappuis confirmed that in the two months he had known Petreman he had been 'a good fellow'. There was insufficient evidence for the case to proceed but enough to put a question mark beside Petreman's name. As a result, he was released but banished. (Sex with a horse was much less common than that with a cow or sheep though a spy arrested in Holland in 1691 confessed to having regularly had sex with horses). A final case comes from 1565, when Mya Leschière had testified that Christophla Leschière (perhaps her sister) had repeatedly told her that Christophla's son, Claude, had had sex with a cow. She knew nothing else about the matter and did not want to say more – though she did know that Christophla had sold the cow.

These cases highlight how very difficult it was to prove an accusation of bestiality. One should not suppose, though, that it was impossible as the next three cases will show. In 1721, a young Catholic named François was caught *in flagrante* with a mare. His master, François Bourgeois (aged fifty), was not a witness to the event but did not doubt what had happened. He testified that he had been brought to the scene by another servant and that the accused had denied he was doing anything but, when called 'a sinful man', he had apologised. The servant, Antoine de Mezière (aged thirty-five), told the whole story. He and Abraham Noviere had been resting on some hay in the stable. Abraham had told him to go and see why the horses were making so much noise. Antoine went on to testify that when he looked he saw François,

> behind a mare with his apron raised, extremely aroused [and the witness] waited a few moments wondering what he should do and saw the said [François] standing on his tiptoes and making all the movements proper to the consummation of his pernicious act, he made some noise. François realising someone was present, put his apron down, cast aside the sack of flour he had been standing on [and] Antoine said to him, '[you] wretch, what you're doing merits being burnt alive'. François trembling all over, responded 'I beg your pardon, Antoine, I wasn't doing anything', [Antoine] said, 'how nothing? I'm going to get the master'.

The case went nowhere as François had had the good sense to flee town while Antoine was off fetching Bourgeois.

Pierre de la Rue in 1617 was not so lucky; indeed, he was extremely unlucky as his case shows. He was arrested in Geneva for various thefts of which he was clearly guilty. The number of witnesses against him was impressive. A couple of them suggested that de la Rue had changed his name from Boccard in an effort to hide his past. Upon further investigation, the authorities were directed to contact magistrates in Beaumont (Chablais). They reported that a man named Boccard had been arrested for, and convicted of, sex with a mare eighteen years before. However, he had broken out of jail before his execution and the court in Beaumont had had to be content with burning him in effigy. Eventually, the authorities were able to link de la Rue with a number of aliases (Jean Passifot, Boccard and La Violette). Under his various names he had been a highwayman who had robbed and injured a number of people. In addition, he had already served ten years as a galley-slave for his crimes. For all of these previous crimes and especially for 'having abandoned himself to committing the horrible and execrable crime against nature with a mare for which he had been jailed [in Beaumont] and had escaped', he was sentenced to death. He met a fate that would have pleased Antoine Mezière a century later – he was burnt alive.

Three years before we have the only case in Geneva that was actually successfully prosecuted by the state. Jean-François Besson (aged twenty-five) was arrested for sex with a cow. Two witnesses gave evidence against him. The first, Bastian Merma (aged nineteen), had been in the village of Pressy the previous Sunday with his master, Pierre Rigot. He had heard a noise from the stable and had looked through a gap in the walls.

> He had seen Jean-François, who had closed the door of the said stable, with his member out of his flies, erect, and, having checked the door, he took a stool and approached one of the cows (named Jaillette) and having moved aside the tail of the said cow he put his member in its ass. [Bastian called another servant, George] to witness the execrable act of the said Jean-François [and] together they had watched him thrusting himself and polluting himself with the said cow.

George Beguin (aged thirty), the other servant, testified that Bestian had woke him up and he had seen:

> the said Jean-François who was standing on a stool and moving so as to pollute himself with a cow called Jaillette having his member in the ass of the said [cow] and he thrust for a long time and he was so shocked to see an act so horrible that neither he nor Bastian had thought to shout out anything to the said Jean-François [to stop him].

Jean-François had not managed to flee because the silence of his witnesses meant that he did not realise he had been seen. He initially denied the charge but when confronted by Bastian and George he confessed that 'he had abandoned himself to committing the horrible and execrable crime of sodomy by copulating against nature with one of the cows which was in the said stable'. He fell on his knees before the court and begged God and the magistrates for mercy saying he had never done anything else like that before. He then begged some more for mercy. The court was not inclined to be merciful and he was drowned.

Societies from the Renaissance to the Enlightenment were not only concerned about sex with animals or various deviations from sex with humans. They also had some very interesting ideas about certain types of human beings. In the first half of the period under examination (to about 1600) there was a widespread belief that the human race was divided into two genders (male and female) but three types of bodies (male, female and hermaphrodite). The last, the hermaphrodite, occupied a place between the two major body types and formed a continuum or bridge between the genders. As such, the genders were not seen as being as distinct as they perhaps are today. In addition, both genders were seen as being part of an overall type which was essentially male. In this scheme, which dated back to Galen, the female body was simply an 'inversion' of the male, the female gender an incomplete or 'failed' male. Female genitalia (bearing in mind the widespread ignorance of the clitoris until the end of the sixteenth century) were male genitalia inside out: the vagina an inverted penis, the ovaries internalised testicles.

In practical terms, this meant that there was a fairly fluid view of gender differences. Biologically women and men were more alike than distinct, with hermaphodites (which were believed to be reasonably common) linking the two. Most hermaphrodites were raised as women and it was illegal for one 'to change' genders at a later stage. This seems to have made it easier for men, in particular, to engage in sexual activities with members of their own sex, especially adolescent males who were not yet 'fully male', lacking a beard. Bisexuality was, thus, socially and culturally more acceptable. As we have seen, the rake of the period was said to have his catamite (adolescent male) on one arm and his whore on the other. Being a member of the 'male' gender was not threatened by sexual acts with males nor by effeminacy.

However, by the end of our period and, in particular, by the eighteenth century these cultural presuppositions had altered. Hermaphrodism was seen as being extremely rare and more often interpreted as a female with an enlarged clitoris. Thus, two bodies were accepted: male and female. At the same time, though, the construction of gender was changing; there were now three (male, female and sodomite). Increasingly, identification with the *male* gender meant specifically avoiding any identification with the behaviour of the *sodomitical* gender. The sodomite became not, primarily, a person who engaged in sexual relations with members of the same sex but a *type* of person with specific characteristics. As Edward Ward wrote in his *The Secret History of Clubs* (1709) there was a,

> Particular Gang of *Sodomitical* Wretches in [London], who call themselves *Mollies*, and are so far degenerated from all masculine Deportment, or manly Exercises, that they rather fancy themselves Women, imitating all the little Vanities that Custom had reconcil'd to the Female Sex, affecting to Speak, Walk, Tattle, Curtsy, Cry, Scold, and to mimick all Manner of effeminacy.

His use of 'degenerated' is interesting because it highlights the extent to which the pre-existing idea of gender and sex as a continuum persisted. The objection against the new gender 'sodomite' was that it was a step backwards in the developmental chain of human existence. That is, men must at all cost avoid 'devolving' into the failed female gender (by behaviour) or sex (by mutilation).

The epitome of this degeneration to the Enlightened mind and, especially, to the British was the eunuch – a 'defect of nature'. These were monstrous creatures who had not only been violently devolved but had compounded the horror by adopting intentionally feminine manners. Their appearance and speech marked them as the very walking, talking definition of the sodomitical gender. Worse, their ability to ingratiate themselves with women, who found their company amusing and the lack of the threat of pregnancy exciting, made them a danger to the established order in which 'real' men dominated women. Also, there was general agreement (amongst men) that the threat of pregnancy was essential for controlling rampant and aggressive female sexuality. In every sense, then, eunuchs were monstrous and the prominence given to them as *castrati* the 'thin end of the wedge'.

It is this view that helps explain the violent reaction that some (male) elements of British society had to the introduction of *castrati* and Italian operas in the early eighteenth century. The sound, nonsense, luxury and effeminacy of Italian society (infiltrating itself into England via the opera) was linked to the bestial. British 'values' of sense, reason, wit and virtue were the marks of 'rational' mankind. As we have seen, the increasing emphasis in the Enlightenment on reason meant that the male was encouraged to shun all qualities (e.g., emotion) which were associated with lack of self control, with being weak and closer to the animals and the flesh. Such things were left to women.

This explains the views expressed by John Dennis in *Essays on the Opera's after the Italian Manner* (1706):

> [Opera has] chang'd our Natures, it has transform'd our Sexes: We have Men that are more soft, more languid, and more passive than Women; [and they wear make-up]... On the other side we have Women, who as it were in Revenge are Masculine in their Desires, and Masculine in their practices.

The ultimate danger of the toleration of these monstrous creatures was the encouragement of the third gender, sodomites, with all their perversions. Dennis warned women, who were great supporters of the opera, that:

> The less will [the men] care for [women], and the more for one another. There are some certain [sodomitical] Pleasures which are mortal enemies to their [female, sexual] Pleasures that past the Alps about the same time with the Opera; and if our [opera] Subscriptions go on, at the frantick rate that they have done, I make no doubt but we shall come to see one Beau take another for Better for Worse.

The satirist Jonathan Swift, writing in *The Intelligencer* (1728), turned the chronology around (while endorsing the view that sodomy was a vice foreign to the British until the late 1600s):

> An old gentleman said to me, that many Years ago, when the Practice of an unnatural Vice grew frequent in *London*, and many were prosecuted for it, he was sure that it would be the Fore-runner of *Italian* Opera's [*sic*] and singers; and

> then we should want nothing but Stabbing or Poisoning,
> to make us perfect Italians.

An anonymous tract of the 1730s was even more blunt. *Plain reasons for the Growth of Sodomy* laid the blame squarely on Italian operas.

The dislike of sodomy and the contempt of Italian society, seen as weak and luxuriant (and, thus, feminine) is apparent. However, there is more to this than just a fear of the general feminisation of society (that is, men). The underlying fear is best expressed by Dryden's translation of Juvenal's *Sixth Satire*,

> There are [those], who in soft Eunuchs, place their Bliss;
> To shun the scrubbing of a Bearded Kiss:
>   And 'scape Abortion.

These men were afraid that, given the choice, their women-folk would prefer sex with these monstrous beings than with 'real' men. *Castrati*, in particular, were seen as creatures 'against nature' and the mere 'shadow' of a man.

The danger was extreme. *An Epistle to the most learned doctor W[oo]d[war]d from a Prude that was unfortunately Metamorphos'd on Saturday December 29, 1722* tells the tale of a woman who had been to hear a *castrato* at the opera. She was so enamoured that when she arrived at home she was overcome by her agitated vapours. So extreme was her reaction that a penis 'fell out of her' and she became an hermaphrodite. This was the ultimate perversion. The mere attraction to such a monster (a degenerate, feminised male) was able to convert a woman into a masculinised deformity – a truly frightening type of monster – a woman with a penis.

No woman was immune to the power of these creatures. The *Plain Dealer* (1724) contained a letter supposedly from a woman seeking advice on her unnatural attraction. She wrote, 'I thought, I cou'd have sworn, I had been Proof against Man; But, alas! – He is not a Man! – He is a being more refin'd'. Fortunately, she had been unable to act on her desires as her inability to speak Italian had proven an insuperable barrier between her and the object of her deviant passions. In 1735, the *Gentleman's Magazine* asked the terrifying question: 'Will [men] suffer their [women], to follow an Eccho of Virility?... Have They no Notion of This more Visible Prostitution, this Adultery of the Mind?' Indeed, so monstrous was the relationship that, at some level, it was almost sodomitical in another way. There was the threat that this was actually the ultimate perversion of lesbianism. *Castrati* were so degenerated as to have become female. Hence, the widely believed rumour in 1736 that the famous *castrato* Farinelli was pregnant.

These monstrous creatures threatened the natural order in so many ways. As feminised men, they were promoters of sodomy and likely to encourage 'real' men into this depraved practice. As semi-women who were (supposedly) able to copulate but without any danger of procreation, they were the ultimate expression of female sexual desire – a living, breathing dildo. Indeed, some sources humorously refer to dildos as 'Farinellis'. (One should not suppose that dildos were that rare either; one French traveller of the 1710s reported that poor women sold them from baskets, disguised as dolls, in St James' park.)

Two quotations from the English translation and adaptation of Charles Ancillon's *Eunuchism Displayed* will suffice to make these points and to bring this discussion to a close. The first denigrates the eunuch as a degenerate creature, a feminised being neither male nor female – not quite human.

> Eunuchs are such, *qui generare non possunt*, as the Civil Law expresses it. Such who can by no means propagate and generate, who have squeaking, languishing Voice, a Womanish complection, and a soft Down for a Beard, who have no Courage or Bravery of Soul but ever timorous and fearful. In a few words, whose Ways, Manners, and Customs are entirely effeminate.

In the second quotation, the English version emphasised their attractiveness to women and their fundamental danger to the right ordering of society.

> However, it is only certain than an Eunuch can only satisfy the Desire of the Flesh, Sensuality, Impurity, and Debauchery; and as they are not capable of Procreation, they are more proper for such criminal Commerce than perfect Men, and more esteemed for that Reason by lewd Women, because they can give them all satisfaction without running any risk or danger.

In effect, not only did eunuchs – these degenerate creatures – encourage sodomy, but they provided women with the possibility of a sexual freedom otherwise unknown before the invention of the contraceptive pill allowed women control over their own reproduction.

Before turning to examine the final, indeed ultimate, perversion of human sexuality – sex with demons – it seems reason-

able to interject a couple of cases which rather fortuitously
link demonic sexuality with bestiality and with castration (or,
rather, impotence). In 1615, Paul Perrot (aged thirty), from
Burgundy was burned for sorcery and sodomy. He admitted,
without torture, that he had been a witch for ten years. He
had been approached by Satan, whom he recognised on sight,
after having had sex with a mare. Satan had given him some
grease (very likely made from human fats, as we shall see
below) which he had used to kill two small children in
Geneva's city hospital. He said, 'he had on many occasions
committed sodomy with [his] mare (for which he was struck
in his conscience with remorse and cried to God for mercy)
and had thereafter given himself to Satan' and 'he had
worshipped Satan'. His depravity had made him an ideal target
for recruitment as a witch.

About a half a century earlier (1562), Claude des Noyers
was arrested for a life of wickedness including making a man
impotent on his wedding night. The summation of the trial
details his sins. He was a 'curser and blasphemer of His holy
name' and had abandoned all faith early in life. He had robbed
his parents. He had become engaged to one of his father's
chambermaids and used that as a cover for two years of fornication. He had then married another woman in Thorens. He
had had six children by her and 'wasted and dissipated their
substance so that by this means having reduced them into
extreme necessity he had abandoned his said children' with
the result that they were 'by his sins, dead of poverty and
misery as he had known'. He then married another woman.
He abandoned her in poverty and moved on to a serving girl
in the Pays de Vaud with whom he fornicated and then
married. He moved back to his father's house in Geneva with

this girl. He then married another woman. He had robbed his master and even, with accomplices, stolen grain, vegetables and hay from the hospital garden so that they could 'gorge themselves'. He then tried to marry another woman but found out she was about to wed so in spite he got a 'certain powder from a woman recently executed for the crime of sorcery and put it in some wine'. This was to make the groom impotent.

The medical reports on Amyed de Carre, the man afflicted by the potion, were detailed. The three medical practitioners reported that 'he excited himself to ejaculation but when he got near her (his wife) to have sex with her, he became frigid'. Colladon, the legal advisor, noted that the potion was 'a crime and poison very cruel and contrary to humankind'. Also, he said that the doctors had ruled that 'the newlyweds are capable and well-disposed in their members with desire to congress together'. He recommended that the accused be burnt alive. In the end, the city's judges were content to hang him.

These two short cases demonstrates some of the concerns early modern societies had about witchcraft and consorting with Satan. First, there was a close connection between Satan and unnatural sex. Second, among the many powers a witch might have was the power to kill and to make impotent. Bearing in mind the paranoid reaction to *castrati* in the 'liberalising' age of the Enlightenment, this was no small concern. Also, these cases make the point that witchcraft (despite what will follow) was not a phenomenon wholly or uniquely associated with women.

A single case from Geneva also demonstrates the fearsome power of witchcraft relating to children and maternity. Our witch above already spoke of the killing of children with grease. In 1563, Nicolarde Masson, a wet-nurse, was arrested on suspicion of having caused the breasts of another wet-nurse to dry up. She admitted that she had touched the nurse's breast while she was feeding the child but only to see if the infant was asleep. Masson was also aware that the nurse, Benoîte Buffone, had said that from that moment her milk had dried up. Masson simply protested her innocence. Two witnesses who were aware of her family's history in one of Geneva's rural parishes informed the authorities that her uncle Cardo had been executed and his corpse dragged through the streets of the village for being a highwayman, a murderer and a witch. Her aunt, also named Nycolarde (and almost certainly her godmother/sponsor) had also been suspected of witchcraft and had had to flee the locale. Finally, her grandmother had left the village rumoured to be a witch. Despite her family's dubious reputation the court held the verdict 'not proven' and banished her on pain of being flogged should she return.

What one sees in these three cases is the general belief that witches had the power to do evil, malefice. This was the fundamental core of the belief about witchcraft. In England, the accusation of malefice remained the basis for the prosecution of a witch. However, on the Continent and, to a lesser degree, in Scotland, an additional element was added to the understanding of a witch. This was involvement in a personal pact or contract between the individual witch and Satan. This agreement and its associated rituals and initiation rites followed a stereotypical pattern (on which, more below). Before discussing these fanciful activities it is essential to understand how they could become so widespread and feature so prominently in most witchcraft trials on the Continent.

People across the Continent were regularly told, through sermons, official decrees, broadsheets and more general works, exactly what sort of behaviour witches engaged in. This pattern arose from an educated and élite understanding of witchcraft itself. Throughout much of late antiquity and the middle ages, the church had taken the view that witches were simply deluded. That is, their claims to power, to be able to fly, etc., were simply delusions. These characters might be dangerous if they used noxious and poisonous compounds in their potions but beyond that they were basically harmless. Indeed, the identification between a witch and a poisoner, as a criminal, was such that the Latin word for a poisoner, *veneficus*, came to mean witch as well.

Increasingly in the later fifteenth and sixteenth centuries, the views of theologians, scholars, jurists and intellectuals began to change. Increasingly, there was a belief that witches did indeed have access to power beyond what might be expected in the 'natural' world. This was not supernatural power (only God resided outwith 'nature' or creation). Nevertheless, there were realms (the preternatural) where demons, angels, and other beings of power resided who were still part of the created order. The power in this region could be accessed by individuals. Learned men through study and the use of special sciences such as alchemy, numerology, Kabbalism, etc., might make use of these powers. However, they did so by the superiority of their learning.

The unlearned (especially women) might also utilise preternatural powers. They required assistance in doing so since they lacked the learning necessary on their own. In effect, the learned gained power *over* preternatural powers while lesser mortals came *under* the power of the preternatural. Once societies, and especially their leaders, had come to accept that such powers existed and that anyone (by one means or another) could access them, it was necessary to understand how this would work. Clearly, an unlearned person would need help and the most obvious source of that aid was one of the denizens of the preternatural realm. The question then became how the witch or magician attained the knowledge and power they were using. Magicians (the learned) did so by science and study; witches by the aid of the Devil and his minions.

This set the stage for the stereotypical method by which witches were recruited. Usually a person (normally a woman) was mentally unbalanced, hysterical or very depressed (often as a result of the loss of a child or extreme poverty). Satan would then appear to her, frequently in the guise of a large black man. If she said 'Jesus', the Devil would vanish. However, he was almost certain to return. Then, if given a hearing, he would promise the woman money and an end to poverty in return for her loyalty. The proto-witch would then be asked to renounce her baptism and God; thereafter, she would worship Satan as her master. In most cases she was then given a grease or ointment which would allow her to attend meetings of other witches and the Devil – the Sabbath.

At these assemblies a number of stereotypical features appeared. The participants would dance riotously and in an unseemly manner (that is, they would whirl about so furiously as to expose themselves). Sometimes demons might be present as well. They would indulge in a cannibalistic feast, as the caption of an early modern print explained:

Here are the guests of the Sabbath, each with a demon at her side. And the only meat used at this feast is from corpses, the flesh of those who have been hanged, the hearts of unbaptised children, and [meat] from other unclean animals which Christians never touch.

At some point in her initiation, the new witch would be touched by Satan and receive the 'Devil's Mark' (a spot on the body insensitive to heat, cold or pain generally). An orgy would then follow in which the witches would copulate with demons (who were often part goat) and Satan himself. The sex would usually involve the witch submitting to anal penetration. As an end to the ritual, the witches would ceremoniously kiss Satan's arsehole.

The image was as depraved and 'against nature' as possible. Bestiality, cannibalism, sodomy and analingus were practised. The eating of children, in particular, specifically mocked the consumption of Christ in the Eucharist. Cannibalism drew on cultural fears not only about witches but also vampires, werewolves and 'alien, uncivilised' societies which ate people either for food or as part of debased rituals.

Why would this stereotypical pattern appear in confessions during trials? One must remember that no matter how careful the judges were, everyone knew the 'correct' answers to the questions in a witchcraft trial. That is, all questions were leading. While claims to malefice might vary dramatically (and might well be based on actual beliefs by the individual defendant and his/her neighbours), a person knew exactly what to say when asked about Satan. Closely confined, deprived of food and sleep, repeatedly questioned and perhaps tortured, many a defendant simply gave the answers they knew would make the torment (the interrogations) stop. Indeed, the realisation that this process was at work explains why both the Spanish and Roman Inquisitions quickly came to the conclusion that it was impossible to get 'the truth' from an accused witch – and stopped their prosecutions of them.

However, even when most European courts, jurists and judges had accepted that witchcraft, although it existed, was impossible to prove in a court of law, belief in it persisted. Indeed in the modern age, which has seen children's books banned from school libraries for 'promoting witchcraft', one has to wonder why so much stress is placed on the existence of a phenomenon that most people believe cannot be proven. A tract, *The Triall of Maist. Dorrel* (1659), written at a time when witchcraft prosecutions were disappearing across Europe enunciated a possible explanation:

> Athiests abound in these dayes and witchcraft is called into question. Which error is confirmed by denying [exorcism], & both these errors confirm Athiests mightly... If neither possession nor witchcraft, (contrary to that hath bene so longe generally and confidently affirmed) why should we thinke that there are Divells? If no Divells, no God.

The author is stating quite clearly that for him and his spiritual/religious worldview the belief in witches, demons and Satan are an essential corollary to, and underpining of, belief in God.

Crucial to this stereotype was perversion. Witches, usually women, engaged in frenzied sexual activities, giving themselves over to licence and lust. Their bastard children were dedicated to Satan and stolen, unbaptised infants were offered to him for sacrifice and ritual cannibalism. Men and animals were made barren and impotent by these same women. Earlier in our period these dangerous women were pictured as voluptuous, sensual, sexually aggressive women emphasising the perversion of women sexually controlled and restrained by society, religion and, more generally, men. After the mid-sixteenth century, the witch was more commonly seen as a saggy-breasted, dried up, old crone – the very antithesis of the 'good mother' increasingly promoted by society as noted above in the discussion about wet-nursing.

Just as the physical image of a witch changed, so did the place of cannibalism and sexual perversion in the stereotype. Originally, these had suggested the voracious, unfettered sexuality of the aggressive female. In time though, as knowledge of other places (especially the New World) increased, the image became that of the uncivilised 'other' in opposition to the refined and rational European. The witch, in submitting to the sexual deviance of the pact and cannibalism, threatened to 'devolve' European society into a baser form very much as the eunuch and *castrato* threatened individual males with degeneracy. In either case, being buggered by Satan was the ultimate sex crime.

The whole of the foregoing discussion has undoubtedly made clear that societies and cultures from the Renaissance to the Enlightenment were radically different from today. Also that this period was not monolithic and unchanging. Attitudes to sex, especially paederasty, in the Renaissance differed from ideas during the Reformation just as much as presuppositions about gender and sex varied in the Enlightenment from those of previous generations. Still, one must remember that sexual deviance and sexual crimes were serious offences throughout the period. People were executed for all of them. The courts were used, effectively and forcefully, to propagate and sustain a normative type of married 'heterosexuality' very much in the missionary position.

This was not, however, the Victorian age. The rakes and fops of the pre-Enlightenment age would have been hounded out of Victorian society as bizarre deviants and perverts – and would still shock today. Concepts of sexuality that allowed adult men to have sex with adolescent males are alien to our own age. Having said that, where statistics can be gathered and where societies were relatively tolerant towards or lax in punishing sexual deviance, the percentages of men engaged in same-sex acts does not seem as alien, albeit this was largely in a bisexual context. In other words, if one must confront the nature versus nurture argument of homosexuality, the historical record provides a mixed account. Nature may provide the base number of individuals interested in their own sex, but social norms and customs largely dictate how those desires would be expressed and understood.

This whirlwind tour of sex crimes suggests that ideas about sex, gender, sexuality and identity are indeed socially constructed. How one understands who and what one is and who and what one desires is greatly determined by culture in all its many facets. It is probably unhelpful to refer to the Florentine twenty-something having sex with a seventeen year old as 'homosexual' or 'bisexual'. At the same time, these societies did have an understanding that some people preferred their own sex almost exclusively, even while strongly disapproving of this and punishing it harshly. If anything, the study suggests that 'nurture' has little impact on those who (for whatever reasons, 'nature' if one will) are exclusively orientated to their own sex/gender. Conversely, it probably has as little effect on those wholly attracted to the opposite sex/gender.

Rather, the study suggests that cultural norms can very profoundly shape how the vast majority who, at one time or another, might find themselves attracted to their own sex/gender respond to those desires and impulses. They might sublimate or deny them. They might channel them towards paederastic relations with physical males not yet 'fully' men. They might adopt an entirely different persona emphasising their rejection of, and differences from, socio-culturally accepted constructions of masculinity and femininity. Finally, this volume has tried to suggest that these cultural presuppositions are fluid over time and that, perhaps, the modern world should consider examining its own presuppositions about sex, gender, sexuality and identity as closely to see to what extent these are expressed as much in response to social norms as in reaction to them.

BIBLIOGRAPHY AND
SUGGESTED READING

Akyeampong, E., 'Sexuality and Prostitution among the Akan of the Gold Coast *c.*1650–1950', *Past and Present*, 156 (1997): 144–73.

Andaya, B. W., 'From Temporary Wife to Prostitute: Sexuality and Economic Change in Early Modern Southeast Asia', *Journal of Women's History*, 9 (1998): 11–34.

Ankarloo, B., ed., *Early Modern European Witchcraft* (Oxford, 1990).

Atwood, Craig D., 'Sleeping in the Arms of Christ: Sanctifying Sexuality in the Eighteenth-Century Moravian Church', *Journal of the History of Sexuality*, 8 (1997): 25–51.

Banner, L., 'The Fashionable Sex, 1100–1600', *History Today*, 42 (1992): 37–44.

Barry, J., Hester, M., & Roberts, G., eds, *Witchcraft in Early Modern Europe* (1996).

Bell, R.M., 'Renaissance Sexuality and the Florentine Archives', *Renaissance Quarterly*, 40 (1987): 485–511.

Binhammer, Katherine, 'The Sex Panic of the 1790s', *Journal of the History of Sexuality*, 6 (1996): 409–34.

Bond, R.B., '"Dark deeds darkly answered": Thomas Becon's Homily against Whoredom and Adultery', *Sixteenth Century Journal*, 16 (1985): 191–205.

Boswell, John, *Christianity, Social Tolerance, and Homosexuality* (Chicago, 1981).

Boswell, John, *The Marriage of Likeness: Same-Sex Unions in Pre-Modern Europe* (London, 1995).

Brackett, J.K., 'The Florentive *Onesta* and the Control of Prostitution, 1403–1680', *Sixteenth Century Journal*, 24 (1993): 273–300.

Brackett, J.K., *Criminal Justice and Crime in late Renaissance Florence, 1537–1609* (Cambridge, 2002).

Bray, A., *Homosexuality in Renaissance England* (London, 1982).

Breitenberg, Mark, 'Anxious Masculinity: Sexual Jealousy in Early Modern England', *Feminist Studies*, 19 (1993): 377–98.

Brown, Carolyn E., 'Erotic Religious Flagellation and Shakespeare's *Measure for Measure*', *English Literary Renaissance*, 16 (1986): 139–65.

Brundage, J., *Law, Sex, & Christian Society in Medieval Europe* (Chicago, 1990).

Brundage, J., *Sumptuary Laws & Prostitution in Late Medieval Italy* (New York, 1987).

Bullough, V., *Handbook of Medieval Sexuality* (New York, 1996).

Bullough, V., *Sexual Practices & the Medieval Church* (London, 1984).

Burg, B.R., ed., *Gay Warriors: A Documentary History from the Ancient World to the Present* (New York, 2002).

Burg, B.R., *Sodomy and the Pirate Tradition: English Sea Rovers in the Seventeenth-Century Caribbean* (London, 1995).

Chajes, J.H., 'Judgments Sweetened: Possession and Exorcism in Early Modern Jewish Culture', *Journal of Early Modern History*, 1 (1997): 124–69.

Clark, Anna, 'Anne Lister's Construction of Lesbian Identity', *Journal of the History of Sexuality*, 7 (1996): 23–50.

Cohn, S., *Women in the Streets: Essays on Sex & Power in Renaissance Italy* (Baltimore, 1996).

Cook, Blanche Wiesen, '"Women Alone Stir My Imagination": Lesbianism and the Cultural Tradition', *Signs*, 4 (1979); 718–39.

Coward, D.A., 'Attitudes to Homosexuality in 18th Century France', *Journal of European Studies*, 10 (1980): 231–55.

Crawford, J., 'Attitudes to Menstruation', *Past & Present*, 91 (1981): 47–73.

De Welles, Theodore, 'Sex and Sexual Attitudes in Seventeenth-Century England: The Evidence from Puritan Diaries', *Renaissance and Reformation*, 12 (1988): 45–64.

Dekker, Rudolph M., 'Sexuality, Elites, and Court Life in the Late Seventeenth Century: The Diaries of Constantijn Huygens, Jr', *Eighteenth-Century Life*, 23 (1999): 94–109.

Desens, M., *The Bed-Trick in English Renaissance Drama: Explorations in Gender, Sexuality & Power* (Oxford, 1994).

Dixon, L., *Perilous Chastity: Women & Illness in Pre-Enlightenment Art & Medicine* (Ithaca, 1995).

Donegan, J.B., *Women & Men Midwives* (London, 1978).

Douglas, M., *Witchcraft Confessions and Accusations* (London, 1970).

El-Gabalawy, Saad, 'The Trend to Naturalism in Libertine Poetry of the Later English Renaissance', *Renaissance and Reformation*, 12 (1988): 35–44.

Ellrich, Robert J., 'Modes of Discourse and the Language of Sexual Reference in Eighteenth-Century French Fiction', *Eighteenth-Century Life*, 9 (1985): 217–28.

Erauso, Catalina de, *Lieutenant Nun: Memoir of a Basque Transvestite in the New World* (Boston, 1996).

Faderman, L., ed., *Chloe plus Olivia: An Anthology of Lesbian Literature from the Seventeenth Century to the Present* (New York, 1994).

Fernandez, André, 'The Repression of Sexual Behaviour by the Aragonese Inquisition between 1560 and 1700', *Journal of the History of Sexuality*, 7 (1997): 469–501.

Feroli, Teresa, 'Sodomy and Female Authority: The Castelhaven Scandal and Eleanor Davies's *The Restitution of Prophecy* (1651)', *Women's Studies*, 24 (1994): 31–49.

Fleischer, M., '"Are Women Human?" – The debate of 1595 between Valens Acidalius and Simon Gediccus', *Sixteenth Century Journal*, 12 (1981): 107–20.

Folbre, Nancy, '"The Improper Arts": Sex in Classical Political Economy', *Population and Development Review*, 18 (1992): 105–21.

Fudge, Erica, 'Monstrous Acts: Bestiality in Early Modern England', *History Today*, 50 (2000): 20–25.

Gerard, Kent & Hekma, Gert, eds, *The Pursuit of Sodomy: Male Homosexuality in Renaissance and Enlightenment Europe* (London, 1989).

Gilbert, Arthur N., 'Buggery and the British Navy, 1700–1861', *Journal of Social History*, 10 (1976); 72–98.

Gilfoyle, T.J., 'Prostitutes in History: from Parables of Pornography to Metaphors of Modernity', *American Historical Review*, 104 (1999): 117–41.

Goldberg, J., ed., *Reclaiming Sodom* (London, 1994).

Goldberg, Jonathan, 'Sodomy and Society: The Case of Christopher Marlowe', *Southwest Review*, 69 (1984): 371–8.

Goodich, M., *The Unmentionable Vice: Homosexuality in the later medieval period* (Oxford, 1979).

Gowing, L., *Domestic Dangers: Women, Words & Sex in Early Modern London* (Oxford, 1996).

Griffiths, Paul, 'Meanings of Nightwalking in Early Modern England', *Seventeenth Century*, 13 (1998): 212–38.

Guicciardi, Jean-Pierre, 'Between the Licit and the Illicit: The Sexuality of the King', *Eighteenth-Century Life*, 9 (1985): 88–97.

Hartman, Janine C., 'The Modernization of the Bourgeois Erotic Imagination in the 18th Century', *Proteus*, 6 (1989): 16–21.

Haselkorn, A., *Prostitution in Elizabethan & Jacobean Comedy* (Oxford, 1983).

Hester, M., 'The Dynamics of Male Domination using the Witch Craze in 16th and 17th Century England as a Case Study', *Women's Studies International Forum*, 13 (1990): 9–19.

Hester, M., *Lewd Women & Wicked Witches* (London, 1992).

Higgs, D., *Queer Sites: Gay Urban Histories since 1600* (New York, 1999).

Hitchcock, T., 'Redefining Sex in 18th Century England', *History Workshop Journal*, 41 (1996): 72–90.

Hopkins, L., 'Touching *Touchets*: Perkin Warbeck and the Buggery Statute', *Renaissance Quarterly*, 52 (1999): 384–401.

Hotchkiss, V., *Clothes make the Man: Female Cross-Dressing in Medieval Europe* (New York, 1996).

Hurl, Jennine, '"She being bigg with child is likely to miscarry": Pregnant Victims Prosecuting Assault in Westminster, 1685–1720', *London Journal*, 24 (1999): 18–33.

Hurteau, Pierre, 'Catholic Moral Discourse on Male Sodomy and Masturbation in the Seventeenth and Eighteenth Centuries', *Journal of the History of Sexuality*, 4 (1993): 1–26.

Huussen, A.H., Jr, 'Sodomy in the Dutch Republic during the Eighteenth Century', *Eighteenth-Century Life*, 9 (1985): 169–78.

Kelly, Joan, 'Early Feminist Theory and the *Querelle des Femmes*, 1400–1789', *Signs*, 8 (1982): 4–28.

Klaniczay, G., *The Uses of Supernatural Power* (Cambridge, 1990).

Kowalski-Wallace, Beth, 'Shunning the Bearded Kiss: Castrati and the Definition of Female Sexuality', *Prose Studies*, 15 (1992): 153–70.

Krekic, B., '*Abominandum Crimen*: Punishment of Homosexuals in Renaissance Dubrovnik', *Viator*, 18 (1987): 337–45.

Kritzman, L., *The Rhetoric of Sexuality & the Literature of the French Renaissance* (New York, 1991).

Krysmanski, Bernd, 'Lust in Hogarth's *Sleeping Congregation* – Or, How to Waste Time in Post-Puritan England', *Art History*, 21 (1998): 393–408.

Kuznesof, E.A., 'Sexuality, Gender, and the Family in Colonial Brazil', *Luso-Brazilian Review*, 30 (1993): 119–32.

Labalme, P.H., 'Sodomy and Venetian Justice in the Renaissance', *Tijdschrift voor Rechtsgeschiedenis*, 52 (1984): 217–54.

Larner, C., *Witchcraft & Religion: The Politics of Popular Belief* (Oxford, 1984).

Lehfeldt, Elizabeth A., 'Ruling Sexuality: The Political Legitimacy of Isabel of Castile', *Renaissance Quarterly*, 53 (2000): 31–56.

Lehmann, A.C., *Magic, Witchcraft, & Religion: An Anthropological Study of the Supernatural* (London, 1985).

Leinwand, Theodore B., 'Redeeming Beggary/Buggery in *Michaelmas Term*', *English Literary History*, 61 (1994): 53–70.

Leites, Edmund, 'The Duty of Desire: Love, Friendship, and Sexuality in Some Puritan Theories of Marriage', *Journal of Social History*, 15 (1982): 383–408.

Levack, B., *Witch-Hunt in Early Modern Europe* (London, 1995).

Lochrie, K., McCracken, P., & Schultz, J., eds, *Constructing Medieval Sexuality* (New York, 1997).

Loughling, M.H., '"Love's Friend and Stranger to Virginitie": The Politics of the Virginal Body', *English Literary History*, 63 (1996): 833–39.

Macdonald, M., *Witchcraft & Hysteria in Elizabethan London* (London, 1991).

Maclean, I., *Renaissance Notions of Women* (New York, 1980).

Maurer, Shawn Lisa, 'Reforming Men: Chaste Heterosexuality in the Early English Periodical', *Restoration: Studies in English Literary Culture 1660–1700*, 16 (1992): 38–55.

McFarlane, Cameron, *The Sodomite in Fiction and Satire* (New York, 1997).

McGeary, Thomas, '"Warbling Eunuchs": Opera, Gender, and Sexuality on the London Stage, 1705–1742', *Restoration and Eighteenth Century Theatre*, 7 (1992): 1–22.

Meem, Deborah T., 'Eliza Lynn Linton and the Rise of Lesbian Consciousness', *Journal of the History of Sexuality*, 7 (1997): 537–60.

Merrick, J., 'Sodomitical Inclination in early 18th Century Paris', *Eighteenth Century Studies*, 30 (1997): 289–95.

Merrick, Jeffrey & Ragan, Bryant T., Jr, eds, *Homosexuality in Early Modern France* (Oxford, 2001).

Merrick, Jeffrey, 'Commissioner Foucault, Inspector Noël, and the "Pederasts" of Paris, 1780–3', *Journal of Social History*, 32 (1998): 287–307.

Mitchison, Rosalind and Leneman, Leah, *Sexuality and Social Control: Scotland 1660–1780* (Edinburgh, 1989).

Morrissey, Lee, 'Sexuality and Consumer Culture in Eighteenth Century England: "Mutual Love from Pole to Pole" in *The London Merchant*', *Restoration and Eighteenth Century Theatre*, 13 (1998): 25–40.

Mourão, Manuela, 'The Representation of Female Desire in Early Modern Pornographic Texts, 1660–1745', *Signs*, 24 (1999): 573–602.

Murray, J., 'Agnolo Firenzuola on Female Sexuality and Women's Equality', *Sixteenth Century Journal*, 22 (1991): 199–213.

Murray, S.O., and Roscoe, W., eds, *Boy-Wives and Female Husbands: Studies in African Homosexualities* (New York, 1998).

Oakley, A., *The Captured Womb: A History of the Medical Care of Pregnant Women* (Oxford, 1984).

Otis, L.L., *Prostitution in Medieval Society* (New York, 1985).

Overmyer-Velázquez, R., 'Christian Morality revealed in New Spain: The Inimical Nahua Woman in Book 10 of the Florentine Codex', *Journal of Women's History*, 10 (1998): 9–37.

Pacheco, Anita, '"A mere cupboard of glasses": Female Sexuality and Male Honor in *A Fair Quarrel*', *English Literary Renaissance*, 28 (1998): 441–63.

Park & Daston, 'Unnatural Conceptions: The Study of Monsters in Sixteenth- and Seventeenth-Century France and England', *Past & Present*, 92 (1981): 20–54.

Parker, Graham, 'Is a Duck an Animal? An Exploration of Bestiality as a Crime', *Criminal Justice History*, 7 (1986): 95–109.

Percy, W.A., III, *Pederasty and Pedagogy in Archaic Greece* (Chicago, 1996).

Perdue, Danielle, 'The Male Masochist in Restoration Drama', *Restoration and Eighteenth Century Theatre*, 11 (1996): 10–21.

Perry, Ruth, 'Colonizing the Breast: Sexuality and Maternity in Eighteenth-Century England', *Eighteenth-Century Life*, 16 (1992): 185–213.

Porter, Roy, '"The Secrets of Generation Display'd": *Aristotle's Master-piece* in Eighteenth-Century England', *Eighteenth-Century Life*, 9 (1985): 1–21.

Poska, Allyson M., 'When Love goes Wrong: Getting out of Marriage in Seventeenth-Century Spain', *Journal of Social History*, 29 (1996); 871–82.

Poster, M., 'Patriarchy and Sexuality', *Eighteenth Century: Theory and Interpretation*, 25 (1984): 217–40.

Restall, Matthew and Sigal, Pete, '"May They Not Be Fornicators Equal to These Priests": Postconquest Yucatec Maya Sexual Attitudes', *UCLA Historical Journal*, 12 (1992): 91–121.

Rey, Michael, 'Parisian Homosexuals Create a Lifestyle, 1700–1750: The Police Archives', *Eighteenth-Century Life*, 9 (1985): 179–91.

Richter, Simon, 'Wet-Nursing, Onanism, and the Breast in Eighteenth-Century Germany, *Journal of the History of Sexuality*, 7 (1996): 1–22.

Roberts, A., *Whores in History* (New York, 1993).

Roper, L., 'Prostitution', *History Workshop Journal*, 19 (1985): 3–28.

Roper, L., 'Witchcraft and Fantasy', *History Workshop Journal*, 32 (1991): 19–43.

Roper, L., *Oedipus & the Devil: Witchcraft, Sexuality & Religion in Early Modern Europe* (London, 1994).

Rose, M., *The Expense of Spirit: Love & Sexuality in English Renaissance Drama* (Oxford, 1991).

Rosen, B., *Witchcraft in England, 1558–1618* (Amherst, 1992).

Rossiaud, J., *Medieval Prostitution* (London, 1998).

Roulston, Christine, 'Separating the Inseparables: Female Friendship and its Discontents in Eighteenth-Century France', *Eighteenth-Century Studies*, 32 (1998–99): 215–31.

Rowland, J., *Swords in Myrtle Dress'd: Towards a Rhetoric of Sodom* (New York, 1998).

Rowse, A.L., *Homosexuals in History* (New York, 1977).

Ruggiero, G., *The Boundaries of Eros: Sex Crimes & Sexuality in Renaissance Venice* (Oxford, 1985).

Rushton, P., 'Women, Witchcraft & Slander', *Northern History*, 18 (1982): 116–32.

Santesso, Aaron, 'William Hogarth and the Tradition of Sexual Scissors', *Studies in English Literature 1500–1900*, 39 (1999): 499–521.

Saslow, J., *Ganymede in the Renaissance: Homosexuality in Art & Society* (London, 1986).

Schleiner, Winfried, 'Male Cross-Dressing and Transvestitism in Renaissance Romances', *Sixteenth Century Journal*, 19 (1988): 605–619.

Schlindler, Stephan K., 'The Critic as Pornographer: Male Fantasies of Female Reading in Eighteenth-Century Germany', *Eighteenth-Century Life*, 20 (1996): 66–80.

Senelick, Laurence, 'Mollies of Men of Mode? Sodomy and the Eighteenth-Century London Stage', *Journal of the History of Sexuality*, 1 (1990): 33–67.

Sharpe, J., *Instruments of Darkness: Witchcraft in England 1550–1750* (London, 1996).

Siena, Kevin P., 'Pollution, Promiscuity, and the Pox: English Venerology and the Early Modern Medical Discourse on Social and Sexual Danger', *Journal of the History of Sexuality*, 8 (1998); 553–74.

Smith, B.R., *Homosexual Desire in Shakespeare's England* (Chicago, 1994).

Sommerville, M., *Sex & Subjection: Attitudes to Women in Early Modern Society* (London, 1995).

Stewart, A., *Close Readers: Humanism & Sodomy in Early Modern Europe* (New York, 1997).

Stone, Donald, Jr, 'The Sexual Outlaw in France, 1605', *Journal of the History of Sexuality*, 2 (1992): 597–608.

Stone, Lawrence, 'Libertine Sexuality in Post-Restoration England: Group Sex and Flagellation among the Middling Sort in Norwich in 1706–07', *Journal of the History of Sexuality*, 2 (1992): 511–26.

Tannahill, R., *Sex in History* (London, 1980).

Teasley, David, 'The Charge of Sodomy as a Political Weapon in Early Modern France: The Case of Henry III in Catholic League Polemic, 1585–1589', *Maryland Historian*, 18 (1997): 17–30.

Terraciano, Kevin, 'Crime and Culture in Colonial Mexico: The Case of the Mixtec Muder Note', *Ethnohistory*, 45 (1998): 709–45

Tóth, I.G., 'Peasant Sexuality in 18th Century Hungary', *Continuity and Change*, 6 (1991): 43–58.

Traub, Valerie, 'The Perversion of "Lesbian" Desire', *History Workshop Journal*, 41 (1996): 19–49.

Trumbach, Randolph, 'Sex, Gender, and Sexual Identity in Modern Culture: Male Sodomy and Female Prostitution in Enlightenment London', *The Journal of the History of Sexuality*, 2 (1991): 186–203.

Trunback, Randolph, 'London's Sodomites: Homosexual Behaviour and Western Culture in the 18th Century', *Journal of Social History*, 11 (1997): 1–33.

Turley, H., *Rum, Sodomy, and the Lash: Piracy, Sexuality, and Masculine Identity* (Chicago, 1999)

Turner, J., *Sexuality & Gender in Early Modern Europe* (New York, 1993).

Van der Meer, Theo, 'Tribades on Trial: Female Same-Sex Offenders in Late Eighteenth-Century Amsterdam', *Journal of the History of Sexuality*, 1 (1991): 424–45.

Vanita, R. and Kidwai, S., eds, *Same-Sex Love in India: Readings from Literature and History* (London, 2000).

Wall, Wendy, '"Household Stuff": The Sexual Politics of Domesticity and the Advent of English Comedy', *English Literary History*, 65 (1998): 1–45.

Walsham, A., 'Witchcraft, Sexuality, and Colonization in the early modern World', *Historical Journal*, 42 (1999): 269–76.

Warnicke, Retha M., 'The Eternal Triangle and Court Politics: Henry VIII, Anne Boleyn, and Sir Thomas Wyatt', *Albion*, 18 (1986): 565–79.

Weed, D.M., 'Sexual Positions: Men of Pleasure, Economy and Dignity in Boswell's London Journal', *Eighteenth Century Studies*, 31 (1997/98): 215–34.

Willen, D., 'Gender, Society and Culture, 1500–1800', *Journal of British Studies*, 37 (1998): 451–60.

Willis, D., *Malevolent Nurture: Witch-Hunting & Maternal Power in Early Modern England* (Ithaca, 1995).

Wright, J.W., and Rowson, E.K., eds, *Homoeroticism in Classical Arabic Literature* (Oxford, 1997).

Yarbrough, Anne, 'Apprentices as Adolescents in Sixteenth Century Bristol', *Journal of Social History*, 13 (1979): 67–81.

Young, M.B., *King James and the History of Homosexuality* (London, 2000).

Zika, Charles, 'Cannibalism and Witchcraft in Early Modern Europe: Reading the Visual Image', *History Workshop Journal* 44 (1997): 77–105.

Zorach, R.E., 'The Matter of Italy: Sodomy and the Scandal of Style in 16th Century France', *Journal of Medieval and Early Modern Studies*, 28 (1998): 581–609.

LIST OF
ILLUSTRATIONS

Unless otherwise stated, illustrations courtesy of William Naphy.

INDEX

Bold refers to pages of significance for the entry

Index

DARK HISTORIES

A series of books exploring the darker recesses
of human history

SERIES EDITOR
William Naphy, Senior Lecturer and Head of History
at the University of Aberdeen

PUBLISHED
P.G. Maxwell-Stuart, *Witchcraft: A History*
'Combines scholarly rigour with literary flair'
The Independent on Sunday

William Naphy & Andrew Spicer, *Plague*
'A chilling warning from history' *The Sunday Telegraph*

William Naphy, *Sex Crimes*
'A model mix of pin-sharp scholarship and deep
empathy' *The Guardian*

COMMISSIONED
P.G. Maxwell-Stuart, *Wizards: A History*

Further titles are in preparation

If you are interested in purchasing other books published by Tempus,
or in case you have difficulty finding any Tempus books in your local
bookshop, you can also place orders directly through our website

www.tempus-publishing.com

or from

BOOKPOST, Freepost, PO Box 29,
Douglas, Isle of Man IM99 1BQ
Tel 01624 836000
email bookshop@enterprise.net

9206